Democratic Autonomy in North Kurdistan

The Council Movement, Gender Liberation, and Ecology—in Practice

A Reconnaissance into Southeastern Turkey

Written by TATORT Kurdistan

Translated by Janet Biehl

NEW COMPASS PRESS

new-compass.net

Democratic Autonomy in North Kurdistan:
The Council Movement, Gender Liberation, and Ecology—in Practice
A Reconnaissance into Southeastern Turkey
2013 © by TATORT Kurdistan

ISBN 978-82-93064-26-8
ISBN 978-82-93064-27-5 (ebook)

Published by New Compass Press
Grenmarsvegen 12
N–3912 Porsgrunn
Norway

Design and layout by Eirik Hasvik
TATORT Kurdistan made the map on page 13

New Compass presents ideas on participatory democracy, social ecology,
and movement building—for a free, secular, and ecological society.

New Compass is Camilla Svendsen Skriung, Sveinung Legard,
Eirik Hasvik, Peter Munsterman, Kristian Widqvist, Lisa Roth,
Jakob Zethelius.

new-compass.net
2013

First German edition published by Mesopotamien Verlag, September 2012 as
Demokratische Autonomie in Nordkurdistan: Rätebewegung, Geschlechterbefreiung und
Ökologie in der Praxis. Eine Erkundungsreise in den Südosten der Türkei.

Contact:
Kampagne TATORT Kurdistan
c/o Informationsstelle Kurdistan(ISKU) e.V.
Spaldingstr. 130-136
20097 Hamburg, Germany
e-mail: tatort_kurdistan@aktivix.org
http://tatortkurdistan.blogsport.de
www.isku.org

Democratic Autonomy in North Kurdistan

Contents

Dedicated to the political prisoners who, for attempting to construct a democratic, ecological, and gender-liberated society, are today incarcerated in Turkish prisons.

Translator's Note

In the Arab Spring of 2011, Muslim peoples who had long suffered repression under brutal dictatorships brought their demands for democracy and human rights to the streets and plazas. Their large demonstrations in several places toppled regimes. Commentators around the world, scrambling to see where this movement might be going, pointed to Turkey as a model for democracy in the Middle East. The Turkish republic, led by the AKP, enjoyed its moment in the sun.

Much less noticed, however, have been certainly singularly undemocratic features of the Turkish state. For decades, Turkey has failed to provide the basic recognition of its Kurdish minority that minorities in other countries enjoy, let alone ensure the Kurds' basic human rights. As many as twenty million Kurds live in Turkey, concentrated in the southeast, in what radical Kurds call North Kurdistan. Under a constitution that asserts the nonexistence of ethnic minorities, Turkey has for decades tried to pacify the Kurds through assimilation and, when that failed, brutalize them into submission. Since 1984 the government has been at war with the PKK, the guerrilla organization waging the military fight for Kurdish freedom—which once upon a time meant the creation of a Kurdish state separate from Turkey.

At the same time, the Turkish government has tried to repress even peaceful Kurdish resistance by criminalizing all activism on behalf of Kurdish rights; anyone remotely associated with the Kurdish freedom movement today is prosecuted as a "terrorist." Just since 2009, at this writing, more than eight thousand mayors, city councilors, journalists, pro-Kurdish party members, lawyers, human rights activists, and others have been thrown behind bars, charged with "terrorism" for advocating basic Kurdish rights.

The Kurdish freedom movement no longer advocates a separate Kurdish state; and the new aspiration that has replaced that discarded one are the subject of this book. Since 2005, the Kurdish movement has advocated Democratic Autonomy, the creation of local democracy, in alternative institutions, as promulgated by the imprisoned Kurdish leader Abdullah Öcalan, who was influenced by the writings on assembly democracy and ecology by the American communalist Murray Bookchin. Democratic Autonomy distills wisdom hard earned by generations of leftists.

To break the prevailing media silence, to publicize the state's repression of the Kurdish freedom movement, and to promote Democratic Autonomy, peace and human rights advocates in Germany banded together to form TATORT Kurdistan. (The name means "Crime Scene Kurdistan.") TATORT has campaigned against the German government's weapons sales to Turkey and its military operations there; against the demonization of the Kurdish movement, against Turkish war crimes, and against dam projects, and much more.

In the fall of 2011, a group of TATORT activists journeyed into the Kurdish areas to discover how the theory of Democratic Autonomy was being put into practice. Their interviewees discovered a remarkable experiment in face-to-face democracy—all the more notable for being carried out in wartime. They described what they had found in *Demokratische Autonomie in Nordkurdistan*, published in late 2012 by Mesopotamien Verlag. The book's unpretentious style masks the boldness of its vision and the richness of its description of a rare endeavor in human history: a conscious effort to implement a socialist utopia. It sets a standard for the socialist theory and practice in the twenty-first century.

I hope this translation helps inform the English-speaking world not only about the plight of Turkey's Kurdish minority but also about its aspirations for a radical democratization.

Janet Biehl
Burlington, Vermont, USA
February 9, 2013

A Note on Names and Places

Due to the repression that exists in Turkey, most of the Kurdish activists whom TATORT interviewed are not named. The TATORT group themselves prefer to remain anonymous in order to be able to continue their work.

For political terms used in these pages, please refer to the glossary at the end of the book.

For place names, TATORT used both Kurdish and Turkish names at each instance. For brevity, I have mostly chosen to use only the Kurdish names. For reference, here are the corresponding Turkish names:

Kurdish name	Turkish name
Amed	Diyarbakır
Çelê	Çukurca
Cizîr	Cizre
Colemêrg	Hakkâri
Dêrsim	Tunceli
Êlih	Batman
Heskîf	Hasankeyf
Gewer	Yüksekova
Mêrdîn	Mardin
Rezik	Bağlar
Riha	Şanlıurfa (Urfa)
Şemzînan	Şemdinli
Şikefta	Suçeken
Şirnex	Şırnak
Wan	Van
Wêranşar	Viranşehir

Names of towns and provinces are often the same. For example, Colemêrg is a city located in Colemêrg province.

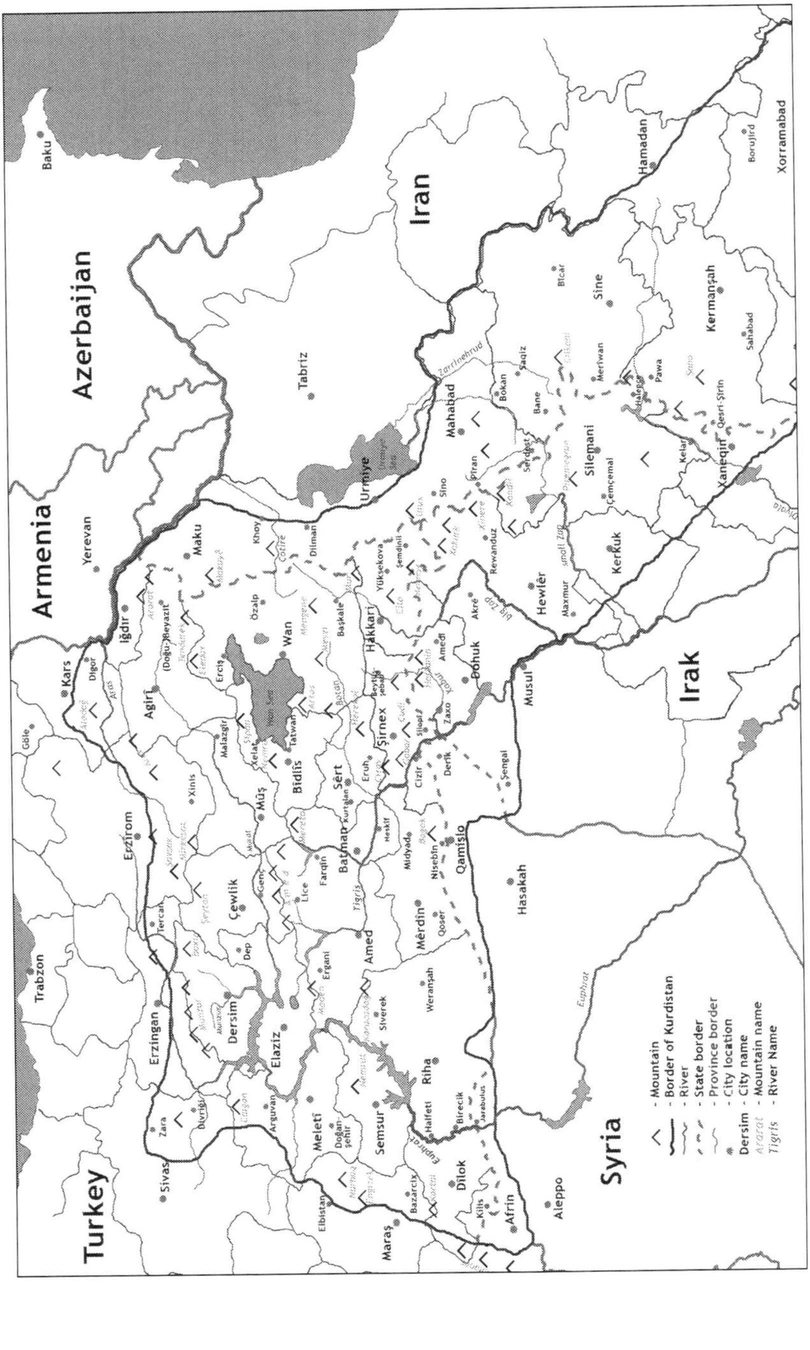

Turkey
Syria
Irak
Iran
Armenia
Azerbaijan
Baku
Yerevan
Tabriz
Hamadan
Borujird
Xorramabad
Kermanşah
Sine
Sahabad
Kars
Trabzon
Erzirom
Erzingan
Sivas
Maraş
Aleppo
Hasakah
Musul
Kerkuk
Hewlêr
Silemani
Mahabad
Urmiye
Wan
Bidlîs
Mûş
Dersim
Elazîz
Amed
Mêrdîn
Riha
Semsur
Dîlok
Afrin
Batman
Sêrt
Şirnex
Hakkarî
Dohuk
Zaxo
Qamişlo
Ağirî
Iğdir
Maku
Çewlik
Tigris
Euphrat
Mountain
Border of Kurdistan
River
State border
Province border
City location
Dersim - City name
Ararat - Mountain name
Tigris - River Name

Foreword

In September 2011 a ten-member group traveled through North Kurdistan (Southeastern Turkey) to study the practice of Democratic Confederalism. Most of the travelers were activists with TATORT Kurdistan. The purpose of our journey was to find out how the Kurdish freedom movement is implementing this theory, Democratic Confederalism, on the ground.

We set out with only a vague idea of how one might go about building a democratic, ecological, and gender-liberated society, let alone in the Turkish part of Kurdistan. What institutions and projects had already been constructed or were under way? What were their main points of emphasis? What difficulties were they experiencing? What were their long-term prospects? These were some of our questions.

During our journey, which lasted ten days, we visited the cities of Amed, Êlih, Dêrsim, Colemêrg, Gewer, and Wan. We had planned our itinerary in advance, but once we were there, we had to stay flexible due to the complications of wartime. All our interviewees were laboring under huge workload and enduring continued repression; some had previously spent time in prison, as part of a wave of arrests that began in 2009. Nonetheless they found time to talk to us.

We recorded most of the interviews, then transcribed them afterward. But especially in Colemêrg and Gewer, our interviewees, concerned for their personal safety, asked us to turn off our recorders and just take notes. That's also why we have not given the names or descriptions of most of the people we interviewed. The Turkish state has criminalized the work of pro-Kurdish activists and civil society groups, forcing them to go underground. Indeed, since our journey, several of our interviewees have been arrested.

Still, this "snapshot" documents a moment in the present situation as well as the practices of the Kurdish freedom movement. We did not cover every aspect of the situation. Even relevant issues, like the possibility of land reform, were not discussed. And much is still being debated internally, as quite a few people observed to us. A deeper analysis would have required a far more structured and lengthy visit.

To us as outsiders, the places we visited seemed quite energized. A civil society counterpower is palpably in place. We hope that these institutions will be able to withstand the Turkish government's harsh repression. They represent an important beginning, even if they have not yet achieved an autonomous existence outside the state and the prevalent economic institutions. But given that Democratic Autonomy has been under construction for only a brief time, and only under conditions of political repression, its practitioners could hardly have achieved much more.

A farther-reaching discussion on the ideas and practice of Democratic Confederalism, building on what we discovered, will be desirable and useful. It contributes new perspectives—even a social utopia—to leftist movements elsewhere.

Enjoy the book!

TATORT Kurdistan

Introduction

Democratic Confederalism

In this chapter, we provide a succinct overview of the ideas that make up Democratic Confederalism. Many aspects that we mention here will be mentioned in the book, sometimes discussed in depth. Here our concern is not to engage with the concept critically but rather to describe it, as it is the ideological orientation for the autonomous institutions that are currently being built.

Democratic Confederalism arose after the failure of Soviet-style socialism and national liberation movements in attempting to create a liberatory society. Starting in the 1990s, Abdullah Öcalan, the now-imprisoned leader of the Kurdistan Workers' Party (PKK), significantly led the Kurdish movement away from the putschist model of revolution and toward a new political direction: Democratic Confederalism, a "democratic, ecological, gender-liberated society." In this development, the writings of the American eco-anarchist Murray Bookchin on social transformation played an important role.[1]

It was a paradigm shift: the Kurdish movement renounced the goal of establishing a socialist nation-state and instead has sought to create a society where people can live together without instrumentalism, patriarchy, or racism—an "ethical and political society" with a base-democratic, self-managing institutional structure that stands in contrast to the demoralizing, homogenizing consumer society of capitalism. This free society is prefigured in the social groups and individuals who are working to achieve it.

When the Kurdish freedom movement originated in the 1970s and 1980s, its emancipatory goal was to create a socialist nation-state, much as other Marxist-Leninist anticolonial liberation movements sought to do. With the collapse of Soviet-style socialism in 1989-90, perspectives changed, and the Kurdish movement underwent an intensive reflection on the role of the nation-state and on state authority in general. Concluding that the nation-state is a construct of bourgeois power in capitalist development, it decided to reject it and attack it politically. It also analyzed the oppressive mechanisms of religion, sexism, racism, and nationalism, which the state requires in order to perpetuate itself.

Capitalist modernity has three basic elements: capitalism, the nation-state, and industrialism. According to the Kurdish freedom movement, the elements of democratic modernity are also threefold: democratic nation, communal economy, and ecological industry. The social system of democratic modernity is Democratic Confederalism, a "nonstatist political administration" or a "democracy without the

---

1   On Bookchin's libertarian municipalism, see *From Urbanization to Cities: Toward a New Politics of Citizenship* (London: Cassell, 1995).

state," predicated on the notion that democracy can flourish only where the state loses its influence.

The first step in the construction of this alternative was the "Declaration of Democratic Confederalism," issued in 2005.[2] Another important step was the "Call for Democratic Autonomy in Kurdistan," dated July 14, 2011.[3] This phase insists that the state respect the democratic will of the population and its need for self-management.

Kurdistan is a mosaic of peoples: Armenians, Assyrians, Arabs, Kurds, Turks, Czechs, Yazidi, Alevi, Sunni Muslims, Jews, and Christians. Democratic Autonomy seeks to guarantee the protection and development of these cultures. Its activists seek to organize all these diverse social groups and identities democratically, by creating councils in the urban neighborhoods and by civil society organizing.

The creation of an operational level where all kinds of social and political groups, religious communities, or intellectual tendencies can express themselves directly in all local decision-making processes can also be called participatory democracy.[4]

The councils are organized horizontally as well as vertically. They reject statist centralism, insisting that decisions must be made by the base. Popular participation generates a politicization of society, in which each person may become an autonomous political actor. The goal

---

2   See Abdullah Öcalan, "The Declaration of Democratic Confederalism," trans. KNK London, KurdishMedia.com. –trans.

3   See "Pro-Kurdish DTK declares 'Democratic Autonomy' in Turkey's Southeast," *Hürriyet Daily News*, July 15, 2011. –trans.

4   Abdullah Öcalan, *Democratic Confederalism*, trans. International Initiative (London: Transmedia, 2011), p. 26. In the quotation, I've changed the word "participative" to "participatory." –trans.

of self-management is to collectively construct institutions outside capitalism, institutions that actively oppose patriarchy, feudalism, and every form of oppression.

> *Ecology and feminism are central pillars. In the frame of this kind of self-administration an alternative economy will become necessary, which increases the resources of the society instead of exploiting them and thus does justice to the manifold needs of the society.*[5]

Another further element of Democratic Confederalism is the principle of legitimate self-defense. Far beyond traditional military defense, legitimate self-defense uses enlightenment and education to defend the achievements of the freedom struggle and organizes the people against attacks by the media and against psychological warfare.

> *Societies without any mechanism of self-defence lose their identities, their capability of democratic decision-making, and their political nature. Therefore, the self-defence of a society is not limited to the military dimension alone. It also presupposes the preservation of its identity, its own political awareness, and a process of democratization. Only then can we talk about self-defence.*[6]

Democratic Confederalism represents a permanent social revolution that is reflected in every area of society. The nation-state will be overthrown over the long term, once institutions of self-organization and self-management are in place at every level. Boundaries, be they state or territorial, will not play a restrictive role, least of all in Kurdistan: Kurdish-populated areas exist in Iran, Iraq, Turkey, and

---

5   Ibid., p. 21.
6   Ibid., p. 28.

Syria. But Democratic Confederalism doesn't regard itself as a model only for Kurdistan.

> *Although in democratic confederalism the focus is on the local level, organizing confederalism globally is not excluded. Contrariwise, we need to put up a platform of national civil societies in terms of a confederate assembly to oppose the United Nations as an association of nation-states under the leadership of the superpowers. In this way we might get better decisions with a view to peace, ecology, justice and productivity in the world.[7]*

---

7   Ibid., p. 31.

1 | Councils Under Construction

The city and neighborhood councils that have so far been constructed—as well as the cooperatives and committees that accompany them—differ strikingly from place to place. But all over the Kurdish region, in diverse geographical, political, and cultural conditions, councils and village communes now exist.

Council building began 2005 and 2006, when so-called "free citizen councils" were organized. Where the base was strong enough, citizens founded neighborhood, district, and city councils. At first the state observed these efforts from a distance, while the European Union, to which Turkey was applying for admission, supported them as advances toward regional autonomy.

In 2008-09 the new councils reorganized themselves as independent structures, to include representation of civil society organizations, women's and environmental associations, political parties, and occupational groups like those of journalists and lawyers.

The pro-Kurdish Peace and Democracy Party (BDP) promoted the construction of these councils, and in the communal elections in spring 2009, the city and neighborhood councils supported the BDP. In these elections the councils demonstrated their organizational strength for the first time. In Amed, Dêrsim, Colemêrg, Gewer, and Wan, at the urging of the councils, the people boycotted campaign events of the Turkish governing party, the AKP (Justice and Development Party).

Thereafter began a wave of arrests that has continued ever since. The so-called anti-KCK operation has criminalized BDP members, mayors, sympathizers, activists on the councils, and the autonomous civil society organizations.[1]

Since July 2011, following the program of Democratic Autonomy, Kurdish activists have accelerated the formation of radically democratic councils. The councils' strength and orientation vary from region to region, depending on political culture, cultural diversity, the influence of religious-conservative groups, urbanization, and state repression. In Colemêrg province the councils are particularly advanced, as they are in the cities of Amed, Colemêrg, Dêrsim, and Wan.

The interviews and reports in this chapter provide insight into the diversity of the councils.

---

1   From 2009 to the present (July 2012), the state has arrested about 8,000 people for alleged membership in the Union of Kurdistan Societies, KCK (Koma Civakên Kurdistanê), under the Anti-Terror Law. Selahattin Demirtaş, co-chair of the BDP, wrote in a letter to Hasan Cemal, journalist and columnist for the newspaper *Milliyet*, that the government knows very well what and who the KCK-ers are (*Milliyet*, February 17, 2012).

1.1   The Democratic Society Congress

The Democratic Society Congress, DTK, was founded in 2005 as a democratic confederation for the pro-Kurdish BDP and other political parties, civil society organizations, religious communities, and women's and youth organizations.

On July 14, 2011, more than eight hundred participants from different tendencies assembled in Amed and issued the Call for Democratic Autonomy, by a common declaration. The published document called for democratic autonomy in eight dimensions: politics, justice, self-defense, culture, society, economics, ecology, and diplomacy.[2] The state promptly criminalized the DTK, as the highest institution of democratic autonomy, and initiated judicial proceedings against it.

In 2005 Abdullah Öcalan had proposed the DTK as a project for the democratic organization of society, as a DTK member explained to us. Its organizers, after holding well-attended discussion forums for a year, organized the first general assembly. We spoke to a member of the DTK about its goals, organizational structure, and specific areas of work:

We intended to bring in a very broad circle of ethnic, political, and religious groups in this general assembly, but because of state repression we couldn't do so at the first meeting. For thirty years our country has been governed by laws dating from the military putsch of 1980. The head of state speaks of the country as a progressive democracy, but it remains a police state. Immediately after its founding, all institutions comprising the DTK were criminalized, and repression was set in

2   See Democratic Society Congress, "Vorlage eines Modellentwurfs für ein Demokratisches Autonomes Kurdistan," January 2011, pp. 30–54.

motion. The repression deterred many dynamic oppositional groups and individuals who wanted to participate in the DTK.

Democratic Autonomy is more encompassing than other theories of autonomy. It uses all the precedents of communal self-government, even the EU's regulations for communal government, as a point of reference. It values positively all instances of regional autonomy, even the federal systems in the European states, which allocate powers to the municipal level and broaden participation.[3] As DTK members explained to us, it's "not just about autonomy—it's about democratic autonomy." It's a matter of the people organizing themselves outside state institutions, and the search for alternatives for communal self-management.

So the DTK, on July 14, 2011, without permission from the state, called for Democratic Autonomy. On the one hand, we are an organization that advocates Democratic Confederalism; on the other hand, we must also cope with the state system. Our foundations aren't the state's laws but civil disobedience and universal human rights. We know the state won't just hand us democratic rights. Moreover the Kurdish question is social and political. So our basis is not the rulers and their institutions, but democratic society and nature. We organize communes in the villages, and councils in the cities, and in that way try to organize democratic self-management.

The DTK's one thousand delegates meet in a general assembly in North Kurdistan. The delegates represent diverse ethnicities, cultures, languages, religious beliefs, and political orientations. Fifteen Kurdish provinces and four west Turkish cities send delgeates to the general assembly. Forty percent of the delegates are elected officials, like

---

3   See for example the 1985 European Charter of Local Self-Government. –trans.

representatives, mayors, and such. The remaining sixty percent come from the grassroots and are elected secretly in a public general assembly. They may be members of women's councils or village communes or they may be unaffiliated persons.

The general assembly, which meets twice a year in Amed, elects a standing committee of 101 people. This committee is presided by five people, which organizes the committee and is responsible for drawing up an agenda. The general assembly also elects the two co-executives of this standing committee. At present they are Ahmet Türk and Aysel Tuğluk.

In addition, there is a coordinating council, which consists of fifteen people and works in three areas: ideology, social affairs, and politics. An array of committees, based on these areas, have been established by the neighborhood councils and city councils. The politics area, for example, has a Committee on Municipal Government and a Religion Committee; the social affairs area has the Youth, Women, and Language Committees.

Within the DTK as well as the city councils, a forty percent gender quota prevails: that is, the proportion of women to men may not fall below forty percent. In some areas women are actually better represented than men; in other areas the reverse.

Kurdish society is patriarchal and dominated by Islam, but the Kurdish revolution is in great part a revolution of women. So in many areas women are more active than the men, far more out in front, and the men are reduced to the second rank. Turkey's rulers feel so disturbed by this development that in the mainstream media they often say we send women to the front ranks as shields.

The DTK has a constitution, we learned, one that doesn't follow the laws of Turkey but is based on democratic participation.

The coordinating council meets every Monday and deals with the social, political, and cultural problems that have arisen during the week. It then works on weekly, monthly and semiannual planning. The standing committee meets every three weeks, discusses the coordination's planning, makes decisions, and sees to it that these decisions will be implemented. When a theoretical decision must be made, the standing committee forwards it to the general assembly. Even if there are no theoretical or strategic decisions to be made, the standing committee calls the general assembly every six months, in order to pass its work and that of the standing committee on to the people.

There are other committees too. The Diplomacy Committee, for example, is responsible for maintaining relations with European countries. That doesn't mean it initiates ambassadorial contact with the French or British state; rather, it builds relationships with people there on the basis of solidarity. The Diplomacy Committee makes quarterly and yearly plans and then goes to Europe to work on implementing them—if it can raise enough money for the plane tickets.

As a specific example of the DTK's work, one of our interviewees described the arbitration of blood feuds. DTK members try to end a blood feud before it can escalate. But they avoid the state courts; instead they discuss and hopefully solve the problem peacefully, within the community.[4]

A practical example: a man called me up and shouted, "My wife has left me—I'm gonna kill her! Bring her back, or I'll kill her!" I tried to talk him down over the phone, but when I couldn't, I went over to his place. We talked for a long time, but I couldn't get him to see reason. Now, I had been married for twenty-five years. I finally told

---

4   See 1.5, "Another Way of Administering Justice."

this man, "My wife also left me. Should I kill her? Yesterday we had an argument. I hit her, and so she left me. Was she right, or am I right?" He thought about it, then hung his head and apologized. Now, don't get me wrong—that never really happened between me and my wife—I just told him it did.

We work with conversation, dialogue, negotiation, and when necessary, criticism and self-criticism. When someone does something wrong, the party who perpetrated the harm has to make it up to the people he injured. We accomplish a lot that way. There's no death penalty, we don't put perpetrators in prison or penalize them financially. Instead, we use social isolation. Relationships with people freeze up, until the person acknowledges the mistake and corrects it.

I was mayor for a year, during which time I was a delegate to the DTK. I've seen many cases of blood feuds and honor killings, for which the state has no solution. We stepped in and, because we better understand people's sensitivities, we were able to solve the problem. I could tell you about innumerable cases like that. Many of our mayors and delegates face such situations. They do these individual interventions, but every locality also has a peace committee, from the BDP or the DTK, that tries to mediate conflicts.

1.2   The Amed City Council

The activists and organizations who take part in Amed's district and neighbhorhood councils and associations come together in Amed Kent Konseyi, the Amed City Council. It is part of the DTK. Every large city in Turkey has a city council, but not all of them are structured for base democracy. What's unique about the Amed City Council is that it is made up of the mayor, the regular municipal government, and various organizations, societies, and NGOs. Decisions are implemented, with the city government taking responsibility. We interviewed several members of the coordinating committee of the Amed City Council.

Who sits on the city council?

It works specifically in the social, political, and ideological areas. Currently we're talking about adding an ecological area and an economic area—in other places these have already been created. The city council now includes representatives of the women's organization, the youth organization, and the political parties. The executive committee forwards the planning done in the city council to the districts, and it then transmits the results from the districts back to the city council. It's the bridge between the district councils and the city council. Amed has thirteen districts, and each one has a council with its own board. Within the districts there are neighborhoods, which have neighborhood councils. Some districts have as many as eight neighborhood councils. And some places have councils even at street level. In the nearby villages, there are communes that are tied to the city council. So power is articulated deeper and deeper into the base.

How do people get on the city council?

People can run for election to a council seat from a district. Every district sends someone to the city council for each area—religion, economy, gender. The diwan is the small executive of the city council, which includes the co-mayor of the municipal government, a representative from the political party in power—currently the BDP—delegates from the civil society organizations, and someone from the city council. All different groups have representation on the city council. There are firm quotas related to the size of the organizations and their strength.

The whole council here in Amed consists of five hundred people. Among them are the elected parliamentarians from Amed, the mayors, and of course those elected to the municipal government in the Turkish structure. Why "of course"? When issues or questions arise in the districts, the delegates here have to have someone to talk to about them. Naturally representatives from the city council have to handle problems that come from the districts and bring them to the city council.

What is the city council's relationship to the mayor, the municipal government, and the other political parties?

The city council tries to include every political dynamic of this city, including the mayor, who has a seat on the council, and all the political parties. Ultimately we try to work out solutions to the problems of the city. Everyone who wants to work with us is heartily welcome. Unfortunately the other political parties tend to have a centralistic mindset and depend on their centralized party organs. So they tend to be uncomfortable with us and reluctant to take part. That's their problem, not ours. But trade unions and other civil society organizations are represented here.

What committees exist now?

Committees exist for the social, political, and ideological areas, and committees for the ecological and economic are under development. The social committees work on education, sports, and health, something like NGOs. They work independently and are in charge of their own self-organization.

The ideological committees work on culture, the press, and the academies. Their prime concern is to popularize and discuss Democratic Confederalism, both with its personnel and at the base. These three parts—culture movement, press, and academies—are organized independently in many cities.

The political area's coordinating committee includes political parties like the BDP, the women's councils,[5] the youth councils,[6] and the municipal and district government. All the committees have a forty percent gender quota.

The economic area is still under construction. Its members come from the DTK and from the municipal government. Currently its main focus is the formation of cooperatives. The work is still relatively inchoate, but it's gradually picking up speed.

What's happening with the cooperatives?

We have cooperatives that grow vegetables and pickle them. Women cultivate mushrooms, or bake bread, to achieve economic

---

5   See 1.3.2, "The Gewer Women's Council," and 1.3.3, "The Colemêrg Women's Council."
6   See Chapter 2, "The Kurdish Youth Movement."

independence. Those are a few of the projects that we have under way. There's also the clay house project, which helps homeless people build clay houses.[7] And communes already exist in many rural places, with the goal of providing for themselves.

What do the legal committees do?

When we talk about judicial matters, you have to understand that we're trying to organize a society without a state. Many people who have legal disputes or other problems that need solving don't go to the Turkish courts anymore—they come to the city councils. So many of the city councils are developing legal committees to handle legal issues, and people are learning to rely on them to solve their problems.[8]

What do the culture committees do?

They're trying to make sure Kurdish language and culture, its literature and music, continue to exist and develop. Kurdish culture is part of human history and its right to exist is anchored in the United Nations Charter. But Turkey doesn't honor this right.[9] We boycotted the schools for a week because of Turkey's one-language education system and actually its one-language life. It accepts only the Turkish language. But we affirm that in this region a second language must be established. We did this boycott, but the press didn't cover it, and the intellectuals and commentators didn't react to it, let alone solidarize, because they're all are directed by the same central leadership—the country's ruling class. With Democratic Autonomy, our goal is to contest precisely this

---

7   See 3.1, "The Ax û Av Cooperative in Wêranşar."

8   See 1.5, "Another Way of Administering Justice."

9   See 6.6, "Mesopotamian Culture Center in Colemêrg," and 6.7, "The Kurdî-Der Language Center in Amed."

centralization and precisely this monopoly of power. We want to expel domination and power relations from social life altogether. And to break this monopoly of power, we have to transfer the authority to make decisions to the grassroots institutions and to the councils.

How widespread is self-organized Kurdish-language instruction?

We're determined to set up self-organized Kurdish instruction in every city. We haven't yet met that goal, and so we're not satisfied with ourselves. But then, we're still, practically speaking, in the first phase. We've made the decision, and now we're trying to implement it.

1.3   The Councils:
The Heart of Democratic Autonomy

To implement a truly grassroots system of democracy, councils must be organized from the bottom up. In this section, we'll talk about the practical work of the councils. We'll look at both women's councils and mixed-gender councils. We attended many council meetings and met with representatives, among others, of a district council in Wan and of women's councils in Gewer and Colemêrg.

1.3.1   A District Council in Wan

We're in a small community center in a quiet district in the city of Wan, far from the large commercial streets, and we're talking with a group of four or five middle-aged men.

How is your council organized?

> *About 15,000 people live in our urban district. We have street councils, district councils, and city councils. When a street council can't solve a problem, it's passed to the district council. If the district council can't solve it, nor the city council, it's discussed in the DTK. Wan has thirty-one districts, five of which have a council. Our work is highly collective and communal, and so we're always considering things in terms of the other districts.*

How many people choose the councilors? Do they get into conflicts? What social structure does your district have?

You know that the state exerts great psychological pressure on the Kurdish population and tries to intimidate it. So many people don't dare to come to assemblies. In summer they work, but in winter they have more time to participate. We organize the People's Congress in the summer—not so many people came at first, only about a thousand. But they elected their sixteen district council members. When we met to establish an association, more than half the district's population turned out. Ours is a democratic people's association, so the Turkish media portray it very negatively, but the association wants to work according to the principles of Democratic Autonomy. A few of our community activists are wanted by the police because of their supposed membership in the KCK. Our last executive committee chair was arrested for that reason. He was freed, but legal proceedings against him continue.

What projects are going on here in the district?

We have a lot projects in mind, but we have many difficulties implementing them, not least financial problems. We want to hold children's language classes, but we lack space. We have the same problem for the cooperative women's bakery that we want to build.

Do you receive outside financial support?

That wouldn't fit our ideology. We're autonomous, so we don't accept financial support. Instead, we assess our district's needs. Are there problems with the water supply or the streets? When we identify a problem, our city council speakers tell the municipal government about it. Solving it is the job of the municipal government. If it has the means, it solves the problem; if it doesn't, it doesn't. But we don't get financial support from the municipal government.

Do you have a women's council here? Is there a women's quota?

We have a women's quota of forty percent, but at the moment we're talking about raising it to fifty percent so that we have real equality. Our executive committee has three women. We don't have a women's council, but we're going to start one next week. We're also going to create a youth council. We're still in the construction phase. But our greatest problem is the ongoing arrests. Our experienced people keep getting arrested, so we continually have to recruit and train new people to fill in the gaps. The state is trying to extinguish the Kurdish movement through the anti-KCK proceedings.

What else does the district council do? Does it get involved in quarrels between neighbors or in cases of domestic violence, when the street councils can't solve those problems?

We have a committee where district people can bring their complaints, yes, like domestic violence and quarrels between neighbors. Let's say a family can't afford to pay for a child's school uniform, or some parents don't want to send their daughter to school. They come to us.

Is the work we do sufficient? you ask. Of course it's not—we could do more. But we have another problem to grapple with. When neighbors in conflict come to us for a solution, the state notices and starts watching us.

Other areas in which we work are unemployment and providing support for people who have financial problems. The goal is always to get them involved in social activities and to actively reconfigure the society.

Do you face state repression?

Even though we're a registered association, one morning, when no one was here, the police smashed the windows and doors of our community center and stormed in. The police called our friends to let them know, but when they arrived, they were arrested. Around the time of the elections, one friend was arrested because of his activities in the community center. Whether his arrest had to do the anti-KCK proceedings isn't clear. His wife is also politically active in our community—she's on the BDP board in Wan. But she now has to cease her political activities, because neither she nor her husband has any financial reserves, and she has to go to work.

When I mention financial problems, I'm not trying to gain your sympathy—it's just a reality here. Our villages were razed, forcing us to move into the cities. We don't know what city life is like or how you're supposed to live here. One friend here had a thousand sheep back in the village and employed fifteen people. Then his village was destroyed and along with it those jobs. Due to the forced relocation into the cities and modern capitalism, an extreme individualism prevails here. And we have to deal with it.

Still, people have seen what the movement has been accomplishing to date, and what it could still achieve. So interest in it is growing.

1.3.2   The Gewer Women's Council

The progress in creating councils varies depending on the district and the local population. The women's councils are a dynamic element— they're doing a lot to change the society's feudal and patriarchal values.

The district of Wan called Bostançi has a robust council movement. The women's councils here are especially strong. Campaigns with slogans like "We're no one's spouse—our spouse is our freedom" and "Let us make a free society and defeat the culture of rape" sharply challenge the social institutions that are entrenched by Turkish dominance.

Another focal point of the women's councils is educational work—literacy, vocational training, and health—as well as bolstering women's self-awareness and discussing the social problems of the patriarchal system. Due to the high level of organization in Bostançi, the women's councils are able to punish perpetrators of domestic violence by socially excluding them. They actively challenges structures of male dominance. The use of quotas and the educational work have set in motion a profound transformation in the council system.

To find out more about the work of the women's councils, we interviewed activists in several cities, like this representative of the women's council in Gewer.

How did an independent women's council emerge here in Gewer?

Around 1996, we organized a women's committee within the erstwhile left-Kurdish party HADEP.[10] We were strongly tied to the party, which we realized was a problem, so we began to work as a separate arm, although still connected to the party. We organized the top first and then filled in the lower structures. Only in 1999 did we start organizing the base.

Now with the women's council it's different. First the base organized itself in 2000, and then the rest came together above it. The council

---

10   The People's Democracy Party, HADEP (Halkın Demokrasi Partisi), was founded in 1994 and banned in 2003. It was a forerunner of today's BDP, the Peace and Democracy Party.

works independently. Women's councils exist in the neighborhoods and the village communes. Ours is city-wide. Ultimately we want a women's council based in each street, but for now that's not happening.

There's also a council for the region—the women's council of Colemêrg.

Gewer's women's council lacks continuity because of all the many arrests. Now our focal point is to create and defend Democratic Autonomy. Once we do that, Democratic Autonomy can stand as a model for Turkey and for the whole Middle East.

What is your praxis?

First we go to the women and ask for their ideas and what their needs are. Then we bring all we've heard to the council. There decisions are made about what to do about them—what kinds of projects will be initiated, or where women's shelters can be built. Then more project ideas emerge, such as for the construction of kindergartens and cooperatives.

We have financial problems—we don't have enough money for all the projects. We apply to places, like the EU, that are willing to fund construction in the southeast. But the Turkish ministries have to approve. So far in this region, only one project has been accepted.

How do you reach out to women?

To strengthen women's participation in the councils, we hold women's assemblies in the city, where we talk about their problems. We try to impress on them that they have to organize themselves to solve their problems. That's the only way they can mobilize.

Can you give a specific example of your work?

The councils try to solve everyday problems. Suppose a woman is having economic difficulties and her house is falling apart. The council decides to help her. The aid will be financial, but also material and practical. If a woman is sick as well as broke, the council may also decide to give her financial assistance. For a case of violence against a woman, the district council tries to find a solution or brings the case to the BDP. The women's councils are not actually institutionalized, and sometimes they're overruled. But the goal is to establish them as a strong institutional base. But unfortunately women who develop strong ideological principles tend to be arrested right away.

How are you organized?

The Gewer women's council comprises sixty percent people's representatives and forty percent representatives of unions and associations. The delegates from the district councils get their mandate for the city council by election. In the summer the work is delayed because many families go to the villages and so can't participate.

Do you intervene in existing institutions?

When the women's council was first organized, we set up a Male-Female-Equality Committee in the municipal government. Whenever women organize themselves, men obstruct, so this committee is important. The Equality Committee also does educational work for men, to develop men's consciousness.

One of the paradigms of Democratic Confederalism is ecology. Is that one of your concerns?

All the women's associations have ecology committees, because women must also have a say about ecology. It's not just a question for men. The issue of gender liberation is also an issue of ecology. One ecology project is tree-planting. Last year three thousand trees were planted, this year four thousand, in five years it'll be a million trees.

Do your projects try to provide economic independence for women?

There just aren't many areas where women can work, so there aren't enough sources of income for them. But however difficult economic independence is to achieve, it's essential for the liberation of women.

We're organizing a women's cooperative in agriculture and animal husbandry. The application has been accepted, and we've been trying to find the right piece of land—as long as we don't have one, the cooperative can't be built. At the moment one woman is employed and twenty-one more will participate. The goal is to have five hundred women working there. First we'll build up the livestock breeding, then the farming.

Next year we're planning to set up a handicraft cooperative, where 150 women will embroider, sew, knot carpets, and such. Our cooperative for agriculture and animal husbandry was the first one in Turkey to be established by a municipal government. But as I've said, because of the missing land, the work is somewhat delayed.

What obstacles do you face?

One problem here is drugs and drug dependency, which affect many young women and children. When their children become drug addicts, the mothers are affected. A rehab center is being developed.

Another problem in this region is that polygamy is permitted. Plural marriage is a form of psychological violence. So we've proposed the following law to the municipal government: If a man takes a second wife, then fifty percent of his wealth must be paid to the first wife, and she is removed from the family,

What is distinctive about Gewer?

Most of the women have been affected by the war—by rape as much as by the death of children. But the women of Gewer have also developed a culture of resistance. Their social participation is relatively good compared with other places. Here you'll find relatively few veiled women. Women in this region can articulate their demands more clearly, because they're politically more educated.

The women's movement is always the target of repression. Do you experience that here?

Last year we organized a campaign against rape culture. Now we're being prosecuted because of a speech someone made at the demonstration. One of the worst acts of violence against women is to forbid them to speak. So we insist on speaking in demonstrations—and in Kurdish, our native tongue. We've been arrested many times because of our Kurdish-language speeches or banners at demonstrations. One female mayor initiated many women's projects. When she was arrested, the projects were discontinued.

1.3.3   The Colemêrg Women's Council

In the small Kurdish city of Colemêrg, we met with members of the women's council. Some of us had been in contact with women's councils here for the previous five years. At one time or another, the Turkish state has suppressed the councils and arrested their members. But every time that happens, a new women's council is founded, as was to happen the day after our visit.

Tomorrow the Colemêrg Women's Council will be founded anew. How has this come about?

The goal of the women's councils is to be able to work independently. Previous ones have been dissolved through repression and arrests. How long women's councils elsewhere have survived, I can't say.

In the Kurdish areas women's political activity is important, and everywhere public opinion favors women's liberation. But it's challenging for women to be politically active. Too often women are victims of violence, both domestic violence and violence from the state.

Another problem is that most of the older women can't read or write. So it's hard to educate these women politically. Today many Kurdish women have finished school, but they get married right afterward. They soon become mothers and get caught up in familial problems. That makes it extremely difficult for them to enter into political life.

How are the women organized in the Colemêrg's districts?

Every district must have a women's committee, so that problems can be addressed quickly. When problems arise in a marriage, local women notice it quickly. Such problems can prevent women from leaving their houses. But compared with women in the big cities, women in Colemêrg are much more active and courageous. Every committee consists of ten or fifteen women. The committees function within the framework of the district councils.

What do the committees do?

If a woman's neighbor is a victim of violence, she notifies us. She comes to us, not to the state, because people have had bad experiences with the state. And we try to find solutions. One woman moved from her village to the city, after which her husband injured his foot. So he can't work, and they have financial problems. We provided food for them, then we talked to the municipal government, which allocated bricks and sand, so they could build a house. We reported the family's problem to the muhtar (the district mayor). We give the same kind of support to women whose husbands are in prison.

Another example: divorce is not accepted here, but we are firmly opposed to domestic violence. When we know that a women has been beaten, we sit down with her and find out what she wants to do about it. Sometimes she loves the man very much and doesn't want a separation. In that case, we call in the family and the husband for a discussion. We explain to him our attitude toward violence and present him with the woman's demands.

If people are to take our movement seriously, they have to take our demands seriously. That's also true when the woman prefers to separate, and she has to return the gifts she received at her wedding, and the dowry. During the period of the divorce, we stand with her.

Have you contacted all the local women?

Yes, we've spoken to almost all the women in the districts—educated and uneducated, unionized and not, all categories. Only the civil servants keep a low profile as far as organizing goes, which they have to do because of their jobs.

How are you connected to other councils?

As I've said, every district has its women's committee, and the city women's council includes two members of the municipal council. Their task is to bring the ideas, wishes, and demands of the women's council to the municipal council. The gender quota in the municipal council is unfortunately not fulfilled. That's because of what I talked about before, the obstacles to women becoming politically active in this region.

Are there conflicts between the women's institutions and the councils?

The women's institutions have been criticized for not developing their ideology far enough. But some of the women can't read or write, and all women bear multiple burdens—they educate the children, they manage the household, and more. And they're also too often victims of oppression within the family. Their leeway for political activities and education is very limited.

1.4   The Dual Structure

Many local governments—in the provinces, districts, and communities—where the pro-Kurdish BDP is in power have been working to construct Democratic Autonomy. A lively exchange of ideas, views, projects, and decision-making processes is under way.

Many municipal governments support the construction of city and district councils, of which they themselves are part or will become part. But the criminalization of the councils is severely impeding official collaboration. Because the Turkish system is so centralized, local governments have their hands tied. The system allots only minimal jurisdiction to the communal level, the financial difficulties are immense, and the social-economic problems in eastern and southeastern Anatolia are onerous.

We sat down with employees of the municipal governments of Gewer and Dêrsim, as well as the mayor of the Sûr district in Amed, Abdullah Demirbaş, to talk about their struggles for communal self-determination and the conditions of their work.[11] A member of the Gewer city government explained:

---

11   Abdullah Demirbaş (born 1966) has written extensively on local democracy and multilingualism. In 2004 he was elected mayor of Sûr, a district in Amed, promising to do the people's business in the Kurdish language. Three years later the Council of State removed him for using Kurdish, Assyrian, and English in providing municipal services. In March 2009 the people of Sûr reelected him to office by an even greater margin, but that May he was arrested once again for links to the KCK and for "language crimes" and was sentenced to two years in prison. He was released in May 2010 for medical reasons. He is currently once again serving as mayor of Sûr. As of July 2012, seventy-four prosecutions against him were under way. See for example "Kurdish Mayor Decries 'Hypocrisy on Language,'" KurdNet, July 23, 2012. –trans.

As the municipal government, we participate in the process of Democratic Autonomy. One of our tasks is to disseminate the concept throughout the society, from the ground up. We support the people in their districts, we organize assemblies, and we discuss how to build Democratic Autonomy, which can be understood as independence from the state. But our first task is to explain it to the people and to mutually enlighten each other.

The Dêrsim municipal government is oriented along the lines of Democratic Autonomy. They mayors have discussed the model many times with the city employees, and they have resolved to build a democratic, gender-liberated, and ecological city. For every task, they ask whether it can be reconciled with this perspective. So dialogue with the people, which they are organizing in the district councils, is crucial. According to a member of the Dêrsim municipal government:

In every district, a council has been organized that refers the district's problems to us. We then go to talk to those individuals affected. Recently we've strengthened the meetings in the districts. Every week the mayors visit the districts and the families who live there. When they visit a family at home, the neighbors come along. Such meetings result in discussions where people can verbalize their problems and expectations.

Our aim is to institutionalize this pattern in the district councils. We haven't done it yet. But we are trying to establish a council in each district, comprising the district's residents. They will discuss local problems and look for solutions or else tell the municipal government what it should do for the district. Such work is being done all over North Kurdistan, but it's developing slowly and not the same everywhere.

Their work together is less a one-sided imparting of information than a conversation among various left groups, especially in Dêrsim, about ways of creating a democratic municipal government. In weekly assemblies, people discuss specific issues, like whether to build a certain road, and general issues, like how to protect nature. Local governments in Dêrsim, Gewer, and Sûr work with priorities that vary greatly.

Sûr, the old quarter of Amed, has a history and culture that is about 7,500 years old. The district government focuses on preserving cultural traditions and Amed's history. Amed has a multiplicity of cultures, ethnicities, languages, and religions. Today Kurds, Turks, Arabs, Armenians, and members of other groups all live there together. The historic city wall of Sûr, 3.5 miles long with eighty-two towers, is being renovated and ought to be recognized as part of the world's heritage. The residents enjoy green and walkable surroundings. Some historic buildings have been restored, and the district government is planning to build a Diyarbakır Museum. It has created a children's library, art and cultural centers, women's centers, and children's festivals. Abdullah Demirbaş described it this way:

I wish to emphasize the diversity of religions and belief systems in this city. Here on Culture Street we've begun to restore a mosque, a Chaldean-Aramaic catholic church, an orthodox Armenian church, and a Jewish synagogue. And we've opened an Alevi and a Yazidi community center there as well.

We're eager to show that people so diverse can all live together in peace. One of the basic projects of Democratic Autonomy is to ensure the coexistence of peoples even with all their differences. When we achieve that, we will have achieved democracy. We're struggling against the official ideology, which says that Turkey has one language, one culture, one nation. But we stand for all things multicultural and multilingual.

The Sûr district government was the first in Turkey to offer services in multiple languages. Its officials speak Kurdish, Turkish, English, Russian, Armenian, and Assyrian. It encourages government employees to speak Kurdish, Armenian, or Assyrian. It promotes linguistic diversity in its projects. For children and families, it's publishing a quarterly magazine and a multilingual book of fables, a fairy-tale book in Armenian, Assyrian, and Kurdish. But these multilingual and multicultural projects antagonize the Turkish state, which creates problems for city employees. Because of his multilingual work, Abdullah Demirbaş was removed from office in 2007. He was reelected in 2009 but then was arrested, and since then he has been persecuted with numerous legal proceedings. Right now the total prison sentences for all his supposed crimes is 232 years.

As the district councils are created, the municipal governments play an ever greater role as the middleman, passing democratic demands upward, while at the same time carrying out a process of democratic transformation. In this dual structure, the boundaries between the allocation of duties and the decision-making processes can become blurred. Said the member of the Dêrsim municipal government:

When we speak of Democratic Autonomy, we can't wait till the laws have changed. We have to make that transformation ourselves, in practical deeds. So a problem may not be part of our jurisdiction, and we may not be paid for handling it, but every problem of the people is actually also our problem. That includes problems that currently come under the jurisdiction of the state. In ten years we will build Democratic Autonomy and make all the decisions that have to do with city planning and its implementation. We'll continue till we implement the whole thing and force Turkey to change its system. But for now we're constructing it de facto. We're concerned now about things that don't belong in our area of responsibility. With the Educational Support Houses,[12] *we're trying to shift responsibility for education from the state. So we're slowly building our own institutions, to develop resistance. We've built youth and culture centers, the first steps toward autonomous cultural work. Turkey has no choice besides Democratic Autonomy—the current system is senseless. History overturns everything that's senseless. The state will be forced to realize this and change!*

In Sûr, the district council makes decisions in collaboration with the city and neighborhood councils. In addition, there's a presidential council and an executive council. The municipal government doesn't interfere with the decisions of the women's councils, which decide autonomously about their budget.[13] Polygamy is not tolerated and in cases of domestic violence, the woman—innovatively for Turkey—receives her husband's salary. The municipal government also created a council for children under eighteen. Abdullah Demirbaş explained:

The children occupied our municipal government and demanded that we put ventilation in the Internet cafés. We agreed and so workers from the town clerk's office went to all the Internet cafés and installed ventilation systems. And we built children's playgrounds according to their wishes and ideas.

The people involved in decision-making overlap between the councils and the municipal government—this must be understood, otherwise the process is incomprehensible. Substantive conflicts are discussed, solutions are devised, and consensus is sought. But if consensus can't be achieved, the issue is decided by a simple majority vote. Demirbaş continued:

12 See 6.5, "Educational Support Houses in Wan."
13 See 4.2, "Communal Projects for Women in Sûr."

You have to consider that we're also members of the city council. Don't think of the city council as separate from the municipal government, because it's not. In meetings we discuss matters of principle and long-term projects. But in such a large decision-making committee, we don't discuss details.

And don't forget that official Turkey doesn't accept this. So when we make a decision, officially it looks as if the municipal government made the decision, but in reality we made it jointly.

In Turkey place names have been changed. So we began a project to restore the old names. First we proposed it to the city council. Then we went to the affected places and asked the inhabitants what they preferred. Ninety-nine percent said they wanted the old names back. That's how the decision was really made, but officially the municipal government made the decision.

The members of the three municipal and regional governments with whom we spoke placed great value on transparency. Citizens should be able to understand what money is budgeted for which project and why at some point the allocated amount no longer suffices. Every few months, for example, the Dêrsim municipal government publishes its current budget, showing its expenditures and its debts, and posts it in the city hall, on its website, and in the local newspapers. Said the Dêrsim municipal employee:

We must be transparent, and the people should know everything. That's part of Democratic Autonomy. Since the city government makes decisions, it has to be accountable to the people. So our city governments subject themselves to democratic controls. There are no such systems elsewhere in Turkey. Every few months our mayor calls a public assembly in the neighborhoods and explains to the people what they've accomplished in the neighborhood, what they're still working on, and what they're planning. Then they ask the people for their wishes. The demands can be general or specific, like "We don't have a road here—build one!" or "A pipe burst here—do something about it!" And every few months, similarly, the mayor calls assemblies of representatives of the local civil society groups. The controls in this system actually lie in Ankara. Every two years Ankara sends an inspector here to check on us. But really, the only thing that should control us is the people. That's why we explain our actions to the people and then listen to their criticisms.

In Turkey's centrally organized system, the powers of local government are very limited. Each of the eighty-one provinces is headed by a governor, who is named by the interior minister and confirmed by the president. This governor is also the head of the elected provincial assembly. Only the mayors and village chiefs are elected by the people. This imbalance of powers between state and local government was very much criticized in our conversations. Said the Dêrsim employee:

All administrative jurisdiction in the provinces is centered on the governor. The governor is not elected but is appointed by the state. The state alone runs the education system, deciding how many teachers will be sent where. And the state makes all decisions about the major transportation arteries, the water supply, cultural issues, and libraries. It makes all the decisions about education and health. It regulates all land ownership, overseeing entries in the land register. On these matters we have no influence. That's unreasonable. Because when something is to be built somewhere, then we examine the site, find out to whom the property belongs, and study whether something could be built there. But only the state institutions can make entries in the land register.

> *The state regulates the judicial system. It supervises journalism. If you want to publish a local newspaper, you have to get permission. Suppose a factory is discharging wastes into the air. The responsibility for monitoring that lies with the state, but it should lie with us. When a factory makes too much noise during its manufacturing process, the governor is supposed to handle it. But that too should be our responsibility. The governor collects taxes from all these areas. The military and police belong to its jurisdiction. They control everything!*

When municipal governments try to change the budget to increase funds for communal work, the Turkish government often obstructs them. So the Sûr district government sometimes just refuses to seek the necessary approvals for loans or other undertakings. Abdullah Demirbaş explained:

> *The Amed mayor's office initiated an enterprise and invested in it. It got all the asphalt it needed for road construction, and it began to hire employees. For next year's budget, the number of employees and the funding were raised. But the government didn't like it and shut down the firm. Every town or city in Turkey has enterprises—out of the sixteen big-city governments, fifteen own and run their own enterprises—but we alone are not allowed to do that. Ankara has four or five million inhabitants, and the municipal government's debt burden is about $4 billion. Amed has one million inhabitants but a debt of only $100 million. In other words, Ankara can incur debt and exercise credit at will, but we can't. Ankara has four times as many people as we do, but they have forty times as much debt as we do.*

The Kurdish provinces are among the poorest in Turkey. According to the Association of Towns and Cities of East and Southeast Anatolia, the region experiences structural economic neglect through minimal investment, inability to obtain credit, and unjust taxation.

Even assistance from outside Turkey is mostly blocked by the state development organizations.

In the city of Gewer, unemployment is about eighty percent. The municipal government has almost no financial means to combat it or other problems, like drugs, prostitution, and smuggling. Ideas and plans for necessary projects are plentiful. But like Dêrsim, Gewer can't get the funding for the urgently needed development efforts like the construction of sewage system or a recycling center, or for social projects like a drug rehab clinic or a women's center.

Near Gewer an airport is currently under construction, but the city government was excluded from the planning process and isn't even sure whether it's being built for civilian or military purposes. A civilian airport would have a positive effect on unemployment, but the city fears that the airport is being built for military use.

Just as it was excluded from planning the airport, the city government had no say in the installation of the surveillance cameras that are everywhere now. Said a member of the Gewer municipal government:

Here in Gewer the economic situation was better in 1993-94. But since 2000 local entrepreneurs have had no income—they earn almost nothing. So unemployment is currently at eighty percent. We're trying to reduce it, but we can't heal this great wound, we can only lessen the pain in a few places. For example we have a project to build a new hospital, for which we need thirty or forty people. So we're trying to fight unemployment in small ways. But we don't think we'll fix the problem anytime soon. Recently the population has been losing all hope.

The central government in Ankara makes all decisions on local government funding. It distributes the funds unjustly, so cities and towns don't get what they need for infrastructure and social projects. According to the Dêrsim employee:

The bureaucracy in Ankara collects tax revenues and gives some back to the local governments. Sometimes it gives less funding to towns where its own party isn't in power and more to those where it is. It just lets our projects hang in the abyss, because it can't abide me. It's told me, "You're a terrorist," and so it blocks our projects.

So many local governments, just to exist, are forced into a gray zone between legality and illegality—and then are subjected to arrests and legal proceedings. The AKP government's wave of arrests against the mayors in Kurdish areas reminds some of the strategy that was used after the 1980s military putsch. Said the Gewer employee:

All Kurdish employees of the city government—including the mayors—the BDP members, the activists, all are being persecuted and arrested. They leave behind gaps that we have to fill. The AKP's goal is to use the strategy that was used after the 1980 military putsch: the military regime imprisoned the mayors and installed soldiers in their place. That is, army members became city governors, holding office till the next elections. Here in Gewer, for nine months in the 1980s, one of these city governors was our mayor. So today the AKP wants to reproduce that strategy and do the same thing.

Another Gewer city employee just wishes to be able to walk the streets without fear.

We want to live a humane and just life, the way people do in Izmir, in western Turkey. There people can go out on the streets at night without fear. We'd like to be able to do that here in Gewer. We've earned such a life. But the AKP policy toward the Kurds is to try to undermine these freedoms and rights.

1.5   Another Way of Administering Justice

*Democratic Autonomy considers a perfect legal system impossible.
Instead of having to choose between ethics and law, it tries to bring
ethics and law into harmony. A society without a conscience is a lost
society; ethics is the conscience and heart of a society's self-government.
We seek to build a system of social justice using the paradigms of
gender liberation, democracy, and ecology.*[14]

The Kurdish population often experiences Turkey's judicial system as
synonymous with exclusion and discrimination. That system ignores
extralegal executions by paramilitary forces, even as it imprisons
Kurdish mayors, journalists, and activists. In the areas we visited, the
Kurdish freedom movement has developed its own judicial system, its
own structures for resolving conflicts. Especially in Colemêrg province,
where Gewer is located, but also in other provinces, people accustomed
to mistreatment and disrespect no longer look to the state-run judicial
system to resolve their disputes.

The development of a self-managed judicial system is especially
advanced in Gewer. We had the opportunity to speak with the legal
committee, a very important and inspiring conversation. The committee
members squeezed us in between two hearings, so we couldn't ask
them anywhere near all the questions that we wanted to ask. They were
not only lawyers but also feminist activists, religious people, political
activists, and others whom the people respect and to whom they turn in
the case of a dispute or offense.

---

14   Democratic Society Congress, "Vorlage eines Modellentwurfs für ein Demokratisches
Autonomes Kurdistan," January 2011, p. 37.

In resolving conflicts, they try to find a consensual solution. Gewer, despite all the progress made by the Kurdish freedom movement, is still marked by strong feudal structures, and cases of revenge and blood feuds are common. The Village Guard system, imposed by the state, fuels the conflicts.[15] Colemêrg province alone has an estimated ten thousand state-armed paramilitary fighters, part of this Village Guard system. Plentiful weapons circulate around the region, and blood feuds escalate, leading to murders and massacres.

The legal committees try to clamp down on this destructive cycle and seek to mediate a peaceful solution between the parties even in cases of murder. When a murder is committed, the perpetrator is punished with a heavy material fine and put on probation. He is also obligated, with the help of a psychologist or other professional, to work on changing the way he thinks about the crime and on taking seriously his punishment. Something similar goes on for those who commit other crimes.

After this punishment process comes the attempt to socially reintegrate the perpetrator. Explained a member of the Gewer legal committee:

Our way of administering justice isn't as retrospective as it is with state systems. We don't lock people up and then release them fifteen years later. Instead we try to effect a fundamental transformation in the person and then reintegrate him.

The legal committees handle cases of domestic violence in such a way as to have an emancipatory influence on society.

The legal committees don't simply handle criminal cases; they also concern themselves with civil conflicts like land disputes. This

---

15 Village Guards are Kurdish paramilitary units that have been recruited, trained, armed, and paid by the Turkish state to fight the PKK.

alternative form of justice is so broadly accepted by Kurdish society that even the state sometimes refers to these institutions. In Gewer they constitute the only relevant judicial system, given the state's waves of repression and arrest. The number of legal proceedings that the courts handle has been plummeting, and even police and other state employees sometimes come before the committee seeking a ruling. This alternative form of justice is clearly successful, as is its underlying humanism, which translates Democratic Autonomy into practice. Nonetheless these new legal committees are being criminalized—many of their members are persecuted by the state.

1.6   Civil Society Associations

To combat the ongoing political repression of the Kurds, the deliberate impoverishment of their areas, and the prevailing feudal subjugation, the Kurdish movement has organized diverse civil society organizations, often integrating them with institutions of local self-government. We present in this chapter three such associations: women opposed to war, people fighting poverty, and the families of prisoners, trying to reduce their isolation. Some of us at TATORT have spent years working with groups like these.

We chose to discuss these associations to represent their diversity, but there are dozens more that are fighting to resolve the Kurdish question and build an emancipatory society in the region. They arise from the many parts of Kurdish society and participate in local self-government, seeking to respond directly to people's needs. The associations have one thing in common: their work has been obstructed by the ongoing arrests and in some cases by extralegal executions. Nonetheless they proceed courageously and continue their exemplary activities.

1.6.1   The Peace Mothers

The Peace Mothers, an initiative of the mothers of Kurdish guerrilla fighters and soldiers, are trying to put an end to the war and advocate a political solution. They aim not only to achieve peace but also to model engaged dialogue as a way of conflict resolution and to advance the democratization of Turkey. But most immediately the Peace Mothers wish to end the bloody military conflict. Even though they have been expelled from their villages and have lost many family members to the war, they welcome the PKK's frequent unilateral calls for cease-fire. They try to call attention to what they call the "Kurdish tragedy" by carrying out actions, attempting to visit politicians in other parts of Turkey and the rest of the world, conversing with intellectuals, writers, and artists, contacting women's associations, and publishing their magazine, *PEACE*.

For years, the Peace Mothers have been holding demonstrations in a central plaza in Istanbul. They have been brutally beaten, arrested, and tortured by the police—as they are when they try to talk to Turkish politicians or military. But that hasn't stopped them from persisting with their peace initiative. Against the background of the current military operations and bombardments, they engage in civil disobedience, attempting, as living shields, to enter the areas of fighting or to occupy party offices, streets, and the like. In the autumn of 2011, they crossed the Turkish-Iraqi border, under fire by the military and police, to recover the bodies of fallen guerrillas. Because of their actions, they are permanently threatened with repression; many of them have spent time in Turkish prisons.

Demands of the Peace Mothers:

1. *An immediate end to all military actions, to protect the lives of children.*
2. *The right to education in the native tongue of all population groups.*
3. *Freedom of press and expression, as a precondition for democracy and tolerance.*
4. *A general amnesty for all political prisoners and for the guerrilla units still in the mountains, as a precondition for peace.*
5. *Termination of the Village Guard system.*
6. *The right of return for those expelled from their villages.*
7. *An end to the repression of civil society organizations, as a precondition for democratization.*
8. *Juridical reappraisal of torture, rape, and murder.*
9. *An account of all those who have "disappeared" after being arrested.*
10. *An end to weapons shipments from Europe.*

In October 2011 we interviewed several Peace Mothers in Amed.

Could you briefly describe your work and introduce yourselves?

"We Peace Mothers want to stop the war so that no more people die and so that no more mothers have to suffer. We go directly to the clash points to show that we don't accept what's happening there."

"No mother wants her child to pick up a weapon. So we would like to contact Turkish mothers and get their support. The Kurds and especially the Peace Mothers say to all Turkey, both the state and the population, that we stand for peace. In the meantime we're willing to risk our lives for peace, as human shields, and we're ready to die along with our children. It's obvious who wants to end the war."

"I don't understand the police today—not only the Turkish police but also the Kurdish and those abroad, in Europe. I'm afraid they're forming an alliance! You begin to think that all these police got their training in the same place."

"We wish we had more international support. When [Prime Minister] Erdoğan or the Turkish state asks for support from other countries, military support, they get it. But when a Kurd wants to go abroad to try to get something for Kurdish affairs, they are prevented. For us, people are people! We don't want any mother to suffer or to lose her child. Yesterday I saw in the news that hundreds of new coffins are being prepared. For whom? Your children and mine! Today ten thousand Kurds live in Europe. They did not leave their beloved homeland frivolously. They fled to that foreign land, so they must bear much sorrow. Most of them had good lives here but had to leave it all behind. No one wants to be away from their homeland for long."

"I ask you, does your country allow the use of chemical weapons? The bombs rain down and burn and choke people. The dead are also maimed, the eyes and ears cut from them. Is it permitted in Europe to pour hot, molten plastic onto the bodies of prisoners? Such things happen here. Europeans consider such things appalling and inhuman, but they're silent about them when they take place in Turkey. And they know very well that they are taking place here. They even sell weapons to the Turks!"

Where did you get the idea of becoming living shields? What were the goals, and how did people react?

"The idea came from us. After the Turkish air attacks began, we sat down together and talked about what we could do. Each one of us shared her ideas. We made our first small attempts at being living shields in 2003 and 2007. The idea came about because we couldn't bear the war any longer. Every morning we heard the Turkish jet fighters over our homes, and every time we nearly died of fright, because we were afraid our children would be killed."

"Do you know, my son is right now in the Turkish military, stationed in Çelê. Last week he was almost killed. We always say that soldiers are our children! We go into these battle areas in order to force both parties to cease fire and to sit down and negotiate. We knew we had to be present and be seen to gain a hearing, because previously our actions produced too little result. When we arrived at the [Turkish-Syrian] border post at Xabûr, soldiers and police surrounded us, and we were encircled by tanks. We couldn't move forward, so we began a sit-down strike on the spot."

"The governor and the gendarmerie came over and asked us who we were and what we were doing. We explained that we came for

peace and that we intended to become living shields between the two parties. But we weren't allowed to go forward. The press came, a few newspapers and a reporter from Roj TV.[16] We explained to them why we were there, that we were mothers on the border and weren't being allowed to proceed. A thousand visitors came and went every day—they didn't sit with us for long. We weren't allowed to have water to wash or food to eat. The press was mostly kept away from us."

"While we were stopped at the Habur border post, we found land mines. We figured out a way to locate and unearth them with our hands, so that no one would unthinkingly walk on them. It went on like this for ten days. A few mothers then went to Kandil and visited other mothers and families there who had lost their children and relatives in the war.[17] We showed them that they were not alone and we expressed our sympathy."

"We've experienced worse. When we recently acted as living shields, someone tried to murder [Peace Mother] Aysel Tuğluk. A young man who had been standing next to her instantly threw himself on her so that the gas grenade hit him instead of her. That very morning this young man had said: 'I will also stand as a living shield for the end of the war.' He came to us to end the spilling of blood, and he died during that murder attempt. They would like to obliterate us."

When did the Peace Mothers emerge? Where is your main office? How do you network?

---

16   Roj TV is pro-Kurdish television network that has since been banned.
17   Kandil is an embattled mountainous region in northern Iraq near the Iraq-Iran border, about 100 kilometers south of Turkey.

The Peace Mothers first came together in 1999 in Istanbul, then in 2001 in Amed. We wanted to register as an association, but the authorities wouldn't let us use the name "Peace Mothers." So we had to present ourselves as "Peace" magazine, but we were actually the Peace Mothers. In the Turkish section, the Peace Mothers have offices only in Izmir and Istanbul. In eastern Turkey we have four more offices. Each Peace Mother is ready to go as soon as we declare an action. The household, the children, the husband—she leaves behind everything when there's an action. Because for us, nothing is more important than peace.

Eleven years ago my daughter tried to burn herself to death. I scolded her and asked her why. I told her that if she wanted to resist, she could find another way. She said that this injustice, this desire for peace and resistance, was very hard to bear. I asked her how I was supposed to cope with her death, if she'd ever thought of me. She said I wasn't the only mother who'd had to cope with such a thing, and that I should instead think about what I could do for peace.

Today Kurdish children have been boycotting their school for five days. For five days I haven't sent my son to elementary school. We aren't demanding anything big. We're only saying that every child has a right to be taught in his or her own language. We don't want our children to have to resist the state. We only want the state to recognize that we aren't going to be silent and that we want our rights.

A few days ago I was up on the balcony with my three-year-old grandson, holding him up. He asked me whether he should throw a stone at the police tank below. I was horrified and asked him why he would do such a thing—the policeman inside is like an uncle to him. Then my three-year-old grandson explained to me that he had seen on TV how the police had shot a young boy. He told me, "If they're allowed to shoot at us, then we can throw stones at them!" What could I say to that child, who could see with his own eyes the injustices that the state perpetrates all around him? I told my grandson: "Please don't throw a stone at the police. Not every policeman is like the one that you saw on TV." We don't want revenge—we want this war and this injustice to come to an end.

How do you think of actions? How do you make decisions? Do you have a leader? Do you meet regularly?

Our meetings take place spontaneously. When a mother gets an idea for an action, or if the political situation, in our opinion, demands an action, then we come together. We also have spontaneous assemblies. We're thirty Peace Mothers in Amed, and when we call such an assembly, then all the mothers show up. Every mother then says what kind of action she envisions or what ideas and concerns she has. Then we vote on the various ideas, and the one that gets the most votes is the one we try to put into action. There's no leader—all the mothers have the same rights and play an equal part in the work. But if we have to give a press conference or an interview, then we decide among ourselves who's most suited to the task. If this mother accepts the role, she performs it, but only once. The next time a different mother will be chosen.

How do you see your work in relation to Democratic Autonomy?

We're getting to know the ideology, step by step, and are trying to apply it from the ground up. The DTK supports us, with its various committees for realizing autonomous self-government. We Peace Mothers are part of this and do our work as best we can. [The Call for Democratic Autonomy] began two months ago, so it's still pretty new for us. For the past two months, we've been studying it intensively. We finally recognized that we can't go to the police or to any state institution with our problems anymore, that the state is what's oppressing us and inflicting most of our problems and injustices. So we want to solve our problems ourselves, in our own society. Democratic Autonomy will take time, but we're proceeding little by little, and I think we'll be successful.

Do you want to explain anything else to us?

We have no wish except for peace. We want everyone who has a conscience to call for peace and do something to achieve it. We're all mothers, whether we're Turks or Kurds. Our skin color may not be the same, and our language is not the same, but the tears that we spill are the same.

We demand that the international media pay attention to the oppression of the Kurds and report on our sorrows. And I appeal to all Europeans to break the silence about the present situation of the Kurds.

1.6.2   Sarmaşık: Against the Deliberate Impoverishment of Kurdish Areas

Sarmaşık is an association that tries to resist the Turkish government's policy of impoverishing the Kurdish areas. The policy is politically motivated—in elections the ruling party, the AKP, bribes people with food expenditures to get its own people elected. Sarmaşık was formed to counter such practices.

Sarmaşık, which means "ivy," was founded in 2005 by sociologists who were concerned about the social situation in the city and province of Amed. They had done a study that showed an alarming connection between war and social need. We spoke with members of Sarmaşık about the war, and how it relates to poverty and the work of the association.

> One of the biggest problems caused by the war is migration, the forced expulsions of people from the villages into the cities. About four million people have had to leave their villages because of the war. About two thousand villages were destroyed. The result of these expulsions is that a large number of people have settled in Kurdistan's big cities, like Amed. Others resettled in the west, especially in the Turkish metropolis of Istanbul. The first thing we did was to develop a municipal plan that showed the city's poor quarters, a "city poverty plan." We divided Amed into four parts and looked for the most affected neighborhoods. In the process, we visited 5,700 households. So the study was comprehensive, and its conclusions were shocking.

> The people were facing not only poverty but hunger. We had to find solutions for this famine. The average annual income in Turkey is $5,000, but in the four poorest neighborhoods of Amed, it's only $240. This gives you some idea of the east-west gap. As a result of the depopulation of the villages in the 1990s, the city's population increased around seventy-two percent. The situation is much worse here than in the villages. Sixty-four percent of the people said that their situation got very much worse when they moved into the city. They said things were much better for them in the villages and that they had no financial problems there. Around fourteen percent of households have a disabled member. Forty-two percent had somatoform disorders. Seven percent of the school-age children worked in order to feed their family and couldn't go to school for financial reasons.

> In Turkey the poverty line is a monthly income of 2,100 Turkish lira per family, and the hunger limit is 740 lira. But in Amed a family often has to make do with only 100 lira per month. In the neighborhoods

we studied, eighty-four percent of the people lived below the hunger line. About 28,000 families in Amed [with an average of seven people] were urgently in need of help. A further investigation into the needs of these people showed that ninety-four percent needed staples like rice, flour, and oil. Two hundred thousand people in Amed needed help with particular urgency. These families lacked basic sustenance.

As a result of this work [on the city poverty plan], we established a Food Bank. That hadn't been the goal of our work, and we hadn't talked about it before. We were just going to study poverty here, to apply numbers to it, and then confront the city. But our findings showed us that we had to set up this Food Bank. It should become a community center in Amed. It was constructed with the help of more than fifty organizations. It supports 2,300 families. This support is not time-limited—it's open-ended, as long as the family's financial situation has not improved.

A sense of solidarity is part of Kurdish culture. As recently as twenty years ago, capitalism didn't have a strong foothold in this province, because the relations of production weren't yet capitalistic. The mentality of solidarity among the rural people is still intact. But with the urbanization of the region and the explosive growth of the cities, capitalism has increasingly established itself and has brought another mentality. The sense of solidarity has lost some of its meaning. Our goal is to strengthen it again.

We're aiming to get to the roots of the poverty in these cities, and we've found that the Kurdish question and the expulsions are the main causes. The state worsens the region's poverty by various means, deliberately. Especially in recent years, as the Kurdish resistance has continued, it has intensified the policy of impoverishment. It functions this way: cause poverty, intensify it, and then make people dependent.

Right after we began our work, we realized that the state and the governor felt threatened—they tried to sabotage our association's work. Even now the governor is trying to prevent us from obtaining office space. We regard our resistance as significant. Even outside Amed people are slowly noticing how valuable such work is. We've now been getting support from abroad, including from Europe.

For in past three months, in addition to running the Food Bank, we've been conducting an education project for children. We give children of displaced people financial aid for their education. You know that the greatest victims of the war are children and women. Children have to work in the streets in terrible conditions and can't go to school. Many can't concentrate on schoolwork because of their poverty. At the moment we're supporting 110 students with stipends. We're especially focused on girls—we support them economically, psychologically, and socially. We follow the children from elementary school to university— we appreciate the importance of continuity.

In a pilot project on health, more than one hundred families who receive support from our Food Bank were given an educational package on women's health, hygiene, and children's health. They also got hygiene aids from us. The women had health checkups, and those who had health problems were sent to specialists. It was a hugely important project, and we would like to restart it with broader support. But for now it's stalled.

For the past year, a professional photographer has been taking photos of the families we support in these poor neighborhoods. Fifty of the photos were selected and sent to academics, intellectuals, and others in Kurdistan and Turkey. They wrote poems or short texts to accompany them. A picture book was compiled from these photos and texts, published in Kurdish, Turkish, and English.[18] *It was sold at various events to raise money for the association. The two photos on the walls here belong to that collection.*

We're trying to publicize every aspect of poverty in Amed, to sensitize people to it and to develop ourselves as an association for solidarity work. The model must be brought against every aspect of poverty, to extend the struggle against it. Poverty is a serious subject. The state and its policies are trying to turn it to their advantage. That's why we have to build an alternative. It's not easy, but it's important to develop a solution.

What is Sarmaşık's organizational structure? How do you propose to create a solidarity center?

Fifteen full-time members work for the association here and in the Food Bank, as well as project groups and volunteers. Some people work half a day or one day per month or per week. All together more than one hundred people work with us on a volunteer basis or else full time.

As to decision-making within the association, we have a board that consists of fourteen people. But each project has its own committee and makes its own decisions, which are approved by the main board. Currently in Amed there are six thousand people who support the association with money and donations. We value steady support, even when it's just a little, since only in that way can we continue the work.

---

18   The photographer was Hüsamettin Bahçe, and the photos were exhibited in 2011 in Amed and Istanbul. The book is called Mazxana, which means "Big House." Thanks to Meral Cicek for this information.—trans.

Do you receive money from other organizations?

We're supported by the teachers' union and the bar association, among others. It's important to extend an awareness of individual responsibility, and to help citizens solidarize with the poor people in this city. We need teachers, lawyers, doctors, people who have a good, regular income, to feel responsible for fighting poverty in their city.

How do you do outreach?

One of our slogans says: "Instead of extending your hands to beggars, let's all join hands." That's how we heighten awareness of social responsibility in people, so they'll support the projects. When institutions support us, they gather their workers or members to explain the Sarmaşık model. So they sensitize people to it. Many of our supporters help fund specific projects. We use volunteers for many tasks. When we ask the institutions for help, they try to organize people.

What's the composition of women and men, and young and old?

It's very mixed—we're not a male-dominated organization. Four women sit on the board, and in other projects the gender dynamics are even more equal. In our work on education, about fifty percent are women. At the Food Bank, a woman is responsible. We see that as very important, because women understand the problems of women better. Our volunteer supporters are especially students and young teachers, although some pensioners work full time for the Food Bank. We have people from all strata. When someone from the board of a bank says he wants to support us, we put a folder in his hand and say, "Go into this poor neighborhood, talk to the families, and make a report for us." It's very mixed, very diverse.

How closely is Sarmaşık tied to the institutions of Democratic Autonomy—the city council and the DTK?

According to Democratic Autonomy, the Kurds are to build their own system with their own energy, meeting their own needs, and solving their own problems. Sarmaşık has a specific role here because the Kurds have an urgent problem with poverty and hunger. The Kurdish people are trying to build their own economic system, in order to be able to solve their economic problems themselves.[19] Of course we're in the middle of a war, which has caused the people and the government great economic harm. During the course of the war, we've seen a transition from a village life based on agriculture, to an urban life. The people have been driven into the cities, forced to migrate there. That's caused the great problem of poverty.

Because of their economic problems, the Kurds are now to a certain extent dependent on the state. Our goal is to break this dependency. This is where our project converges with Democratic Autonomy. Even a poor population can be instrumentalized by the state. We want to deprive the state of this possibility, so that it can no longer use these people. Instead people should have their own way and decide freely in elections.

Politically, the state is losing out here—that's beyond question. And because of the resistance, it's losing militarily, too. The only area in which it's still able to hold sway is the economy. That's why it considers Sarmaşık so dangerous, perhaps as dangerous as a political party. It's trying to ban us. Recently we've been forbidden to rent office space. Maybe the best indication that our work has meaning for Democratic Autonomy is that we've become a target.

---

19   See Chapter 3, "Economic Alternatives."

Do you get any external support from international solidarity groups or associations that do similar work on community empowerment?

> We accept support from individuals abroad, but not from international institutions. That's not a contradiction. Some people feel solidarity with the Kurdish people and want to support a solution to their problem. We consider their support very important. But we don't want any support from the EU, the IMF, or the World Bank. Those are institutions of states, and anything they provide to people in Turkey has to pass through Ankara. But the Turkish state is trying to bring us to heel. Since we're not going to do that, accepting such support is excluded.

> Yes, our focus is on gaining support and solidarity from people within Amed, but we're not opposed to support from outside when they're trying to lend us a hand. Turkey's application to join the EU has brought support money in. But again, there's a problem with distribution. The EU forwards the money to the NGOs—but only through the mediating body of a Turkish ministry. And of course it's not equitably conveyed. Compare the financial support that NGOs in Kurdistan get with what NGOs in western Turkey get. It's laughable. That's really the problem.

In spite of the repression, work seems to continue in Sarmaşık. Some of the participants in our journey, who have been following the work of Sarmaşık since 2008, have observed a very positive development there despite the repression. Sarmaşık has far surpassed the goal it set back in 2008, to help 3,000 to 3,150 people—it now supports more than 20,000. Economic need grows, yet the Turkish government has been obstructing Sarmaşık's work, trying to criminalize it, calling people it helps "terrorists." But Sarmaşık doesn't support people based on their politics—its only criterion is poverty. The "terrorist" accusation shouldn't hinder its work, but it's frightened some people away, and now they're afraid of receive aid. For example, after the October 2011 earthquake in Wan, Sarmaşık initiated a campaign to assist the victims. But in January 2012 the state levied a fine of 862 Turkish lira on every member of its leadership, saying they had broken the law. Furthermore, the state froze 76,000 lira that had been raised to aid the earthquake victims. Such obstacles are set up routinely in the Kurdish areas to block emancipatory initiatives.

1.6.3   Association for Prisoners Support

A prominent aspect of daily life in the Kurdish areas is the danger of going to prison. Under the AKP government, the number of political prisoners in Turkish jails has ballooned. Thousands of Kurdish guerrillas are detained in prisons, and alongside them, as of September 2011, more than five thousand members of civil society organizations, politicians, mayors, journalists, human rights activists, lawyers, and others also languish behind bars.[20] Their sheer number makes work on their behalf indispensable.

The Association for Prisoners Support, or Tuhad-Fed, was founded in 2003 as a federation of several prisoner support groups.[21] With more than ninety offices in dozens of cities, Tuhad-Fed publicizes the fact that political prisoners, "hostages of the Turkish state," are forced to endure mistreatment and unimaginable detention conditions as punishment for their successes in the struggle for Kurdish freedom. Almost all our interviewees have family members who have been murdered, tortured, or incarcerated.

---

20   Since the spring of 2009, more than 8,000 Kurdish political activists have been arrested, most of them members of the BDP and its allied organizations; among them are mayors, city councilors, lawyers, trade unionists, human rights activists, and feminists. See *Dokumentation über die Menschenrechtsverletzungen in der Türkei der letzten Jahren in Zahlen* (Frankfurt: Civaka Azad, Dec. 13, 2012). –trans.

21   Tutuklu ve Hükümlü Aileleri Dernekleri Federasyonu, TUHAD-FED.

Since prisoners don't receive adequate medical care, campaigns are mounted to demand that the Turkish state free sick prisoners. Currently fifty-four prisoners are in mortal danger—their immediate release is vital.[22] In the past three years, at least fifteen Kurdish political prisoners have died due to illness. According to Tuhad-Fed, routine prisoner food does not provide sufficient nutrition; special diets for the sick are unavailable. Efforts to reform prison conditions a few years ago actually only worsened the situation—prisoners were forbidden to accept food brought to them by their family members. That left them entirely dependent on the unhealthy prison food and whatever was available in the overpriced prison stores, which included no fresh produce. Prisoners are forced to perform labor, like painting the prison walls or eliminating mold, without pay. For longtime prisoners, the inadequate nutrition and hygiene lead directly to serious illness.

Prisoners are harassed in other ways as well. According to the Human Rights Association (IHD), when sick prisoners are taken from Amed for treatment in Istanbul, they are transferred more than a thousand kilometers in armored personnel carriers. Human rights activists have much criticized these vehicles as places of systematic attack and torture. The prisoners are transported in handcuffs, from the time they leave their cells to the end of the journey. The armored personnel carriers have no heat or ventilation. Their lawyers consider these transports a form of torture, and they are not alone. The prisoners are beaten, searched, and otherwise mistreated during the transportation. Since they are already seriously ill, this abuse is life-threatening. Demands for gentler forms of transport and care for prisoners is consistently refused.

As a result of the current arrest wave, prisons are drastically overcrowded. In many places, prisoners don't have their own beds

---

22 According to IHD Diyarbakır, the number of critically ill detainees is 306 as of January 27, 2013. –trans.

but have to sleep atop one another in layers. In the E-type women's prison in Bidlîs, thirty-five women and children occupy one cell. For yard exercise, they are allowed an area of about thirteen square meters. The massive overcrowding, the meager food, the brutal assaults, and the general mistreatment injure or sicken prisoners. In F-type prisons, solitary confinement, a form of torture, leads to severe physical and psychological illness and sensory deprivation.[23]

Many human rights and other organizations as well as the pro-Kurdish BDP are working to prevent "death behind bars" and achieve freedom for sick prisoners. But such humanitarian work is dangerous in Turkey—prisoner-aid activists have themselves been incarcerated. Prisoners have also initiated hunger strikes and protest actions, to challenge their conditions.

We interviewed Tuhad-Fed members in October 2011 in Amed.

Can you tell us about Tuhad-Fed and its work?

Our federation consists of nine organizations, and we have more than ninety offices in various cities. We monitor the conditions of more than ten thousand political prisoners, both civilians and guerrillas. We keep track of their health, and we help them write petitions and appeals and fill out bureaucratic applications. We look after their families. We're trying to take responsibility for supporting them in ways that go beyond the material. We organize solidarity actions on behalf of severely ill prisoners. We speak on behalf of prisoners to the outside world. We have carried out protests. A few days ago we organized a

---

23 F-type prisons, authorized by the 1991 Anti-Terror Law, are maximum-security prisons with cells for one to three people. Prisoners are not permitted contact with other prisoners. Older Turkish prisons housed at least fifty people together in dormitories. Human Rights Watch, Amnesty International, the Human Rights Association (IHD), and the Human Rights Foundation of Turkey have all criticized these prisons. –trans.

memorial for ten prisoners who were beaten to death by guards in the Amed prison in 1996. We don't want this atrocity to fade into oblivion.

Another important focus of our work is the situation of Mr. Öcalan. He is the representative of the Kurdish people, and his situation reflects the people's situation and that of all other prisoners. He has now been isolated from his family members and his lawyers for more than a month.[24] Even his five co-prisoners have been barred from visiting him for five months, because in the exercise yard they were speaking Kurdish.

What is the situation in the prisons?

In 2000 the Turkish state, in "Operation Return to Life," established modern F-type isolation prisons. The purpose was to make it impossible for prisoners to use prison time to educate one another and organize. They can do that when they're sitting together in one big space. But when only three or four people are housed in a cellblock and are unable to read or write, they can't educate each other. In smaller groups, prisoners can be isolated more efficiently.

By this means, the state has separated the people and the PKK prisoners. When a family can visit only once a year, so that instead of forty-five minutes of weekly visiting time they now have forty-five minutes yearly, we have reached a whole new dimension. Turkey's application process to the EU meant that prisoners were allowed certain rights on paper, like the right to speak Kurdish. But in practice those rights have been eliminated through disciplinary punishments.

---

24 Öcalan's isolation began in July 2011 and still continues today (November 2013). –trans.

The PKK is not giving up on organizing. The Turkish state may arrest someone and hope to break them. But afterward that person steps forward as even more politicized. And despite the isolation, the prisoners are still organizing themselves collectively. No distinction is made whether a prisoner comes from a rich or a poor family. Money paid into an account for prisoners is administered in common and distributed equally.

Have you at Tuhad-Fed experienced repression?

Of course. We expect to be arrested at any moment. We've just received the statistics for the last three months: 2,316 arrests, 850 imprisonments. Many of our members are in custody. We're under surveillance—our telephones, as well as our offices, are bugged.

How is Tuhad-Fed tied to the institutions of Democratic Autonomy?

We're represented in the city councils. When we want to organize an action, we do it not as Tuhad-Fed but as a council. Other civil society organizations are present there too, like the Union for Internal Refugees,[25] and the Association of Relatives of the Disappeared.[26] Each of these associations has an internal council and a speakers' committee, which they send to the city council. Association members can participate in the councils as individuals as well. Every person in a city neighborhood automatically has the right to bring issues before the council. Anyone who has a problem can bring it to a meeting, and it will be discussed. The council tasks the executive council with implementing the proposed solutions.

25 Göç Edenler Sosyal Yardımlaşma ve Kültür Derneği, GÖÇ-DER.
26 Mezopotamya Yakınlarını Kaybeden Ailelerle yardımlaıma Derneği, MEYA-DER.

1.7   Şikefta: In the Shadow of the Ilisu Dam

Near the small city of Heskîf (Hasankeyf in Turkish) lies the village of Şikefta. Since the end of the 1970s, Şikefta has been organized collectively. Its story is closely bound up with the history of the Kurdish freedom struggle, under the leadership of the PKK.

A special historical development led to the village's base-democratic structure. In 1979 a left-Kurdish revolutionary was elected mayor of the Êlih administrative district, but soon afterward he was murdered by the state. Şikefta village had overwhelmingly supported him. In retaliation, the large landholders inflicted repression on the village population. Twenty-two people died in the clashes.

The people of the village fled to the nearby caves,[27] where they organized a collective way of life. After a while the people came back to Şikefta village. But then came the military putsch of September 12, 1980, and the village was turned into a veritable torture center. The people were systematically threatened and ill-treated. In the 1980s and 1990s the state demanded that the villagers collaborate, working as Village Guards. The villagers refused and began a resistance that continues today. A certain large landowner, who once held sway like a feudal lord, bowed to the popular resistance and left the area.

Then Şikefta was subjected to a food embargo—only a small amount of grain and other foodstuffs could be brought in. Finally, during the repression of the 1990s, many village residents were murdered by state or parastate forces. Nonetheless the village succeeded in further developing itself as a commune. The villagers pooled their income and managed

---

27   Along the Tigris River there are caves providing natural shelter. "Şikefta" is the Kurdish word for "cave."

their lives collectively, on the basis of solidarity. They farmed collectively, in both large and small landholdings. They ran a sand mining operation, in which all workers were insured and received a regular compensation. The village collectively owns a minibus, and a new community center and assembly house will soon be built.

The collective achievements extend beyond matters of the economy and infrastructure. In Şikefta the Kurdish freedom movement, with its emphasis on women's liberation, has led to gender equality, such that Şikefta stands out among other villages in conservative Êlih province. The women villagers say that they have equal rights with the men and that no gender hierarchy exists. They can travel freely without getting permission from their husbands, such as to take part in political actions. Women are a lively presence in Şikefta's streets—they are out in the open. They have equal decision-making rights in the village assembly and have seen to it that forced marriage and polygamy are illegal in their village. When we talked to teenagers in the collective village, they said they prefer life there to life in the city.

But now the village's very existence is threatened by the Ilisu Dam.[28] Should it be built, the dam would flood a large part of the village. It would not only destroy an irreplaceable historical site, it would drive ten thousand people from their homes, and eradicate the socially valuable collective life in Şikefta.

---

28 See 5.2, "Current Environmental Activism."

1.8   A Village Commune near Gewer

In 2007 the residents of a village near Gewer city decided to constitute themselves as a commune, to become a model for the province. They had held many discussions and sought opinions from outside. In the end, three factors proved decisive for them: the prison writings of Abdullah Öcalan,[29] the historical experiences of the Kurdish movement, and European experiences with communal life.

Those in the commune who were willing to take on greater responsibility organized themselves into village councils and began to build the commune. They created several village councils consisted of around 20 to 70 people, depending on the village's size. Most villages in the province have 20 to 120 houses. For 100 houses, 30 or 40 people are represented in the council. Many families choose one person to represent them in the council. At the moment the commune has three speakers, who represent the council to the outside.

Private property continues to exist in the commune—the houses and gardens belong to individual families. What's different now is that no longer only one family owns all the land and decides on its use. The villagers farm many fields collectively.

Establishing this communal use initially encountered resistance. Several families refused to participate and could be persuaded only through the efforts of the city council. But most of the families want to participate in communal life and value its institutions. The prospect of mutual aid was highly appealing. When one woman, a few years ago,

---

29   While in prison, Öcalan has written a series of self-defenses—discourses on history, political theory, economics, nature, and culture—for the European Court. Some of them have been translated and published as *Prison Writings*. –trans.

was in dire financial straits because her husband had been imprisoned, the villagers built her a house.

Today the composition of the village council is diverse, consisting of women, children and men of various age groups. There's no age limitation—seven- and eight-year-olds helped organize the last Newroz celebration.[30] In order to counteract traditional gender roles, a women's quota was set. If not enough women are present, then no meeting can take place.

The village commune has eliminated problems that especially hurt women, like polygamy, physical violence, and exclusion from economic life. Such abuses contradict the principles of a commune. If a man wants to take a second wife, for example, he will be socially isolated. The most severe punishment is expulsion from the village.

The village has established committees for health, economy, sports, and culture. Their members are elected for one-year terms and report on their tasks every six months. In these interim reports, they identify problems and propose solutions, which are to be implemented in the following six months. Someone who doesn't carry out his or her tasks satisfactorily can be removed from office.

Since the founding of the commune and the establishment of the village council, much has improved. Today there are no more cases of polygamy or domestic violence. If such a thing were to happen again, the woman knows she can go to the village council and make the episode public. Initially the council tried to solve complaints about domestic violence through dialogue and consulted the council of elders. But finally the village developed an attitude of disapproval toward violence against women as such.

The poaching of animals and the felling of trees have also been curtailed. The library no longer stocks books about the hardships of

---

30 Newroz is the Kurdish new year, March 21.

village life but instead offers educational opportunities on diverse subjects, from health to Kurdish language to the history of communes. The villagers receive assistance and expertise from outside. Recently a group of doctors instructed individuals on the subjects of first aid and women's and children's health. These lessons serve as multipliers, as the knowledge spreads to other villagers.

The families in the commune can scarcely imagine moving to a city. The landscape may not be the most beautiful, and the village still has problems, but in the commune "life has become meaningful again," says one resident. "Problems can't be solved by the state. We can find solutions for concrete projects, and life can be lived communally through Democratic Autonomy."

2 | The Kurdish Youth Movement

Organizing a Determined Resistance

The Kurdish youth movement is one of the most dynamic parts of the civilian Kurdish freedom movement. Young people organize to protect demonstrators, devise their own political and cultural activities, and receive language education. According to their representatives, about fifty percent of the activists are female. Young women do youth work alongside young men, in mixed organizations, but also in their own autonomous groups. Young people organize resistance and build alternative institutions in all parts of Kurdish society. We met with several representatives of the youth movement, including some from Gewer.

A special focus is cultural activities, meaning music, drama, and film. In theater pieces and sketches, young people challenge sexism and violence and grapple with Kurdish history. Theater groups perform plays urging a basic social transformation in distant villages and set up cultural exchanges there. Young people record stories and songs performed by villagers, to preserve them. They educate themselves politically through reading and discussion groups.

A big problem for Kurdish youth is drugs. State forces distribute drugs in Kurdish areas, especially heroin, in order to weaken the young people's potential for resistance. And drug addicts can become informers and spies for the state, providing it with witness statements and documents. The youth movement tries to counteract this by treating youth for drug addiction, integrating them politically and socially, and if necessary financing a stay in a rehab clinic. It urgently needs money to build a new clinic.

The movement also resists the state's assimilation policy in the schools. Speaking the Kurdish language can mean corporal punishment for a student. Every morning all students are forced to stand in front of the Turkish national flag and swear that they are proud to be Turks. The youth movement organizes boycotts against this practice, sometimes with success. In 2011 they organized a school strike in Gewer—almost 100 percent of the students participated. We discussed these and other important areas of youth work, like self-defense and rebellions, in our interviews.

Because it plays such an important role, the youth movement is perpetually in the cross-hairs of the state. Currently hundreds of young people from Gewer are in prisons. But young people accept the daily possibility of arrest and don't lose heart because of it. Another form of repression that they face is the psychological terror of being tortured and of "disappearing."

On December 10, 2010, on the road between Gewer and Wan, Turkish soldiers stopped a small bus carrying youth movement activists. Among them was the speaker of the Democratic Patriotic Youth (DYG) of Gewer, Sedat Karadağ. The soldiers forced the young people to lie down with their faces to the ground. They roughed Sedat

Karadağ up and finally shot him in the head. He survived but was seriously injured and lost an eye. He is still in custody. His story is not unique—such episodes are routine for the Turkish military.

Gewer is known, as we have seen, for its deep-rooted political organizing—and for the harsh repression its people have experienced. Entering the city center means crossing an unofficial border—state authority can do so only with the help of a large operation. Because the Kurdish movement is so strong here, life is much different from many other cities in the region. Women move around the streets as freely as men, and in spite of the severe repression, the general mood is feisty and self-assured. The youth movement actively pits itself against the state. It sets a remarkable example by protecting demonstrations. It fears neither the state nor the feudal institutions.

We sat down in Gewer to interview a group of young men between sixteen and twenty-six. The young women were absent that day because they had all gone to Amed to attend an important women's conference.

We're glad to be able to speak with you. How did the Call for Democratic Autonomy in July 2011 affect your work?

The Call for Democratic Autonomy meant that we entered a new phase of the resistance. The goal is now to construct institutions of popular self-management, and to widen the cleavage between the Kurdish people and the hegemonic Turkish state.

At the same time students are fighting for the right to speak Kurdish in schools, without bringing down disciplinary punishment. Students refuse to utter the daily oath "Happy is he who can call himself a Turk." And they practice other forms of resistance. We're trying to use Kurdish for formal correspondence like applications and invoices.

What is going on in the schools? We heard something about a school strike.

The most important thing is the struggle to use the Kurdish language. You're right—recently we led a five-day school strike, in which almost 100 percent of the students participated. We demanded that lessons be taught in Kurdish and that textbooks cover Kurdish history and culture. Today the Turkish school system systematically denies the very existence of the Kurds. In the elementary schools, teachers beat children who don't speak Turkish.

I personally had Turkish inflicted on me through violence. Only in the fifth grade was I able to express myself in this language. Moreover the schools demand that we sing the Turkish march and swear an oath to Turkey. Anyone who refuses is expelled. But our school committee is well anchored in the schools, and we have a wide range of action.

The state is trying to indoctrinate Kurdish children at a young age, to prevent them from joining the freedom movement. It separates them from their families as early as possible, requiring children in the Kurdish areas to start school soon after they turn four. Of course we're for an early and comprehensive education. But the Turkish state, to buttress its claim to domination, is abusing the children. For us activists, the most crucial movement education takes place in jail. But the state schools are obviously an important battleground for us. The state does its propaganda openly there, while we do it in hiding.

What role do youth play in the Kurdish freedom movement?

We think young people are the vanguard of social change. They are the least inclined to accept the existing social relations, and their minds are the least imprinted with the Turkish state's structures of domination. Moreover, because of the economic and social realities in which they grew up—war, occupation, repression—they know they don't have much to lose, and so they are the most likely to make sacrifices for the resistance.

What is your relationship to ordinary students?

In general, many youth who sympathize with the movement have a high degree of education. Many study medicine or other academic programs. We appeal to students to think of the Kurdish people and help build communal structures in the villages. But we prefer our committed activists to have a political education rather than follow an academic program of study as lawyers or doctors. A student should have time to dedicate him or herself to the movement.

What institutions do you have, and how do they function?

We've organized ourselves in a council system, according to the principles developed by Serok Apo ["Chairman Abdullah Öcalan"] in Democratic Confederalism. A presidential system is excluded. Up until recently, the youth institutional structure was officially part of the party, but today it functions autonomously. The youth and women's movements are the most advanced component of the Kurdish freedom movement-and we've also implemented Democratic Confederalism most broadly. All the city neighborhoods and the villages around Gewer have youth councils, whose representatives also work in the people's councils. Youth are planning to transform all of Gewer into a self-managed commune. We've divided the city into twenty-seven sectors and are building councils for each one. Youth are the most important factor not only in the uprising, the

Serhildan,[1] and the resistance actions in the streets, but in all areas of social life here in Gewer.

Youth work takes three forms: cultural, social, and resistance. Our cultural work consists mainly of strengthening the local traditions and thereby strengthening popular self-consciousness. We organize theatrical performances on political themes and practice the traditional Kurdish speak-singing, dengbêj. Our social work involves, among other things, providing health care. After demonstrations, organized groups of medical students treat victims of police attacks. We help young people with sports and tutoring. We're working on economic empowerment through collectives and cooperatives, with the goal of strengthening the people's self-organization and so making possible the independence of our institutions from the Turkish state.

The Kurdish freedom movement has achieved great successes in the last thirty years. It has awakened a Kurdish consciousness, one that will not go back to sleep very quickly. At the moment we're moving into a new phase of the revolution through the construction of communes, collectives, and cooperatives. Popular self-organization of the economy has the goal of laying the groundwork for a comprehensive change in prevailing social relations, and of making comprehensible to people perspectives beyond war, poverty, and occupation. The movement is building village, youth, and women's cooperatives. Youth work has gained much dynamism since 2007. Our work has become more public, and it's easier to address the people's various needs. The different levels of self-management let us enter into the process of organizing more easily. Especially work at the local neighborhood level has turned out to be mobilizing.

---

1   Serhildan is the Kurdish name for the resistance movement since the 1990s.

You spoke of self-defense. What do you mean by that?

Youth are the vanguard of the Serhildan. We don't just practice
militant self-defense against police attacks at demonstrations; we also
work offensively against the institutions of the Turkish state.

What kind of cooperatives do you have here in Gewer?

We mainly have cooperatives for animal husbandry and for
agriculture. Young people advise villagers about farming. Our friends
who are engineers and veterinarians can be helpful. In the past we've
helped collect herbs from the fields, but now that the Turkish army
uses chemical weapons, it's no longer an option. So we support the
cooperatives in other ways. We don't have our own youth cooperatives
because we don't want young people to form relationships with one
another through money. They should be the vanguard and the engine
of the resistance. So whenever possible, our cadres are supported
economically by their families.

*We've heard that a lot of drugs are circulating in Gewer. What are your
thoughts about that?*

It's a big problem, along with the repression through arrests. The
state is trying to lure young people away from the resistance by
getting them addicted to drugs. Friends have seen police distributing
heroin and synthetic drugs to young people. Then the police exploit
their dependence and their economic privation to use them as spies.
Prostitution is another growing problem.

In Gewer 3,500 youth are drug addicted. A thousand of them are
still children. The Kurdish youth movement would like very much to
build a drug treatment clinic, but we lack the means. Now we're caring

for fifty drug-dependent young people and are trying to help wean them away from drugs through social action. These young people need therapy, so we help them with that financially. Finally we try to integrate them into Kurdish social and political institutions. We don't abandon them as people. A good way to help would be to build that rehab clinic here in Gewer.

What is life like for young people in Gewer?

War is a routine condition here, shaping people from birth. This province has seen many military operations, partly because the resistance here has always been so strong. Our generation has grown up in this war. Every one of us has a family member who has been killed; some of us have been traumatized by the Turkish military. When I was six, the army attacked my village at three o'clock one morning. Soldiers appeared at the door of every house and drove us all into the village square, humiliating us. So from childhood on we have all been "Apocus" [children of Abdullah Öcalan]. "Biji Serok Apo!" [Long live Chairman Öcalan!] are the first words that many children here utter.

Are the youth institutions open to all young people?

Yes, anyone can join. We have no problems recruiting, since about ninety percent of the population here sympathizes with the movement. Almost every family has a martyr in its ranks. We send male and female delegates to the city council. Young people here in Gewer have their own self-defense units that work independently and need no tutelage from old men.

How do you recruit?

We have different ways. We get contacts through the district councils and also from patriotic and socialistic families. We offer cultural activities, sports, and health education, as well as political education. In all our daily work, we're trying to build trusting relationships with our peers.

How much do women and girls participate in the youth movement? What is your relationship to the Kurdish women's movement?

Along with youth, women have the highest degree of organization in the Kurdish movement, and young women are also the strongest, most self-conscious part of the youth movement. Young women organize mostly alongside young men. But because of our Islamic-influenced society, they discuss subjects like health, hygiene, and sexuality separately from men. And because conservative ideas are still widely held in Kurdish society, often only women can make contact with other women, although this is less of a problem among youth. Discussions of patriarchy and women's oppression are central to our ideology and are a central subject of schoolwork.

What's the relationship between the sexes in your movement?

In the youth movement, males and females organize in common. The proportion is about fifty-fifty. The women among us are militant, autonomous, and radical.

Your region is fairly conservative. Does the state sometimes try to "pacify" it with Islam—for example, with the help of the Gülen movement? [2]

Gewer is located in a geostrategically important place, and the local resistance here is strong. So the AKP government and the Gülen movement are trying to use Islam as a weapon against the women's

---

2   A conservative religious movement founded by Fethullah Gülen. See Glossary.

movement. But their efforts to gain a foothold here have collapsed, as they have not in Êlih and other Kurdish cities. Here we have a center of radical Islamists who've tried to influence popular opinion against the Kurdish movement. But the people don't trust them. They're mostly religious, sure, but they also experience oppression as Kurds, and so they don't want to hear from Gülen or Erdoğan.

Families are still structured along feudal lines, but in recent years much has changed, partly because of the particular strength of the freedom movement in this region. Twenty years ago it was almost unthinkable for a young women to go into a Turkish city to study, but today young women have no such problem. Especially in socialist and Apo-supporting families, the problem has been more or less overcome.

But as a movement we're not opposed to Islam or other religions. We reject the Gülen sect and its ideas about a greater Ottoman empire. And we're opposed to the feudal structures that remain in families. For example, when children are forbidden to go to school for "religious" reasons, we're against it. And we oppose radical Islam, because it's irreconcilable with the values of a democratic ideology. But fundamentally we're open to all religions. Religion is a private affair— what's important to us is democratic ideology.

We've heard that many youth movement activists are behind bars. Can you do anything about that?

In the last six months, 1,372 friends from the youth movement have been arrested, and more than 3,000 total are now in prison, serving sentences from six years to life. We're trying to make contact with their families and their lawyers, but the repression of the Turkish state often makes that difficult. We work closely with the Human Rights Association (IHD) and other civil society organizations. The living conditions in the prisons are often atrocious, causing many people to develop serious and even life-threatening illnesses.

Many of the prisoners were arrested at a very young age and leave jail years later as educated cadre. Prison education is highly esteemed by the Kurdish people, especially by the youth. A few jokingly complain that they haven't yet been arrested and so can't attend "Kurdish university."

What is the situation with the arrested activists?

For the past decade, young people have been routinely singled out for repression. But we use prison time to educate ourselves. Illiteracy remains a serious problem here—it impedes our ability to teach the Kurdish freedom movement about theory. Back in 1994, when I was fourteen, I was arrested and spent seven years in prison. I was detained in a big hall along with about sixty people, and grouped together like that, we were able to give each other an education and have social activities like soccer and dancing.

But the introduction of the F-type isolation cells in 2000 has made that all but impossible. Prison personnel don't torture people physically as often as they used to, but the psychological torture of solitary confinement is much harder to endure. This so-called "white torture" aims to destroy the individual and his or her spirit. In the past the goal was just to destroy your body. Walling us off from the outside takes a gruesome toll on the psyche. Only your political convictions and your belief in the Kurdish revolution will help you endure it.

My time in the F-type prison was the worst I've ever personally experienced. Kurds are very social people. We're seldom alone, spending most of our lives with brothers and sisters, friends, and family. Solitude is onerous for us. But now so many Kurdish activists are in prison that the isolation cells are becoming overcrowded too, and as many as four people occupy in one cell. That's making the educational work possibly even more intensive than it was in the large groups. That's at least one benefit of the Turkish state's mass arrests.

In the German left, the bias persists that the Kurdish freedom movement is nationalistic. How do you respond to that?

We don't consider ourselves nationalists. We're socialist internationalists and are part of a worldwide revolutionary movement. We feel connected to struggles in other parts of the world, from the uprisings in North Africa to the anarchist youth revolt in Greece. But at the moment we're under attack by the Turkish state as Kurds, and so we're forced to struggle on that terrain. Socialism and the anticapitalist struggle are important components of our ideology, but at this moment our oppression as Kurds is our main problem. And while we are socialists, Kurdish society is traditionally organized more along anarchist lines.

3 | Economic Alternatives

As the ten of us prepared for our journey to North Kurdistan, we were acutely aware of the global nature of the capitalist system, and we expected to find whatever alternative models existed to be rudimentary. A "seizure of the means of production" can occur, after all, only in a phase of revolutionary transformation that presently is not on the horizon.

The Kurdish movement can travel the road to construct Democratic Autonomy only one step at a time. Its attempts to create the new are taking place within the old. The projects we visited thus have "only" a transitional character. When we asked about the movement's economic outlook and its views on ownership of the means of production, a member of a political education academy answered this way:

We're not saying we've found the right solution. But we think the system we're trying to develop is as close as possible to the right solution. Much as the West, in the early Renaissance, tried to uncover and revive the values of ancient Greece, today we're trying to uncover and revive old values of the eastern societies. A communal society remains present within eastern societies. The capitalist system is penetrating those societies and developing an unstable foothold there, but communal life and communal ways of thinking persist. Cities are a problem, because cities are the centers of capitalist modernity. Cities enhance individualism and selfishness. So especially in the large cities, its important to transform consciousness, and the academies are trying to do that, to recover the communal system for the Kurds who have immigrated into the cities. But for the cities themselves we have at the moment no good solution.

According to Democratic Confederalism, two principles are necessary for a future economic order: popular participation in all economic planning processes, and collective solutions to these social responsibilities. All further principles—for example, as described in the Parecon proposal of Michael Albert[1]—such as self-management, sustainability, complementary equality, solidarity, diversity, and efficiency, may arise only from these two preconditions.

The projects we visited testify that implementing these ideas is a difficult task.

---

1 Parecon, as defined by Albert, is "participatory economics." See Michael Albert, *Parecon: Life After Capitalism* (London: Verso, 2003). –trans.

3.1   The Ax û Av Cooperative in Wêranşar

Our first example of a cooperative, in the sense that's meant by the Kurdish movement, is the Ax û Av (Earth and Water) Cooperative in Wêranşar, south of Amed. Since 2011, the cooperative has been building collective housing and has generated revenue by raising and selling pickled produce.

We interviewed members of the cooperative in 2011, during the second Mesopotamian Social Forum, MSF, at Sümer Park in Amed.[2] Near where we talked stood a house that ten women and men had collectively built from clay.

Why have you built this clay house here in the park? Does it have a function, or is it a demonstration?

With our Ax û Av project, we're trying to establish a political economy in this region that's based on democratic participation. Our work is represented in the DTK, and of course we're also part of the political movement. We're tied to the regional dynamic and are trying to contribute to the new paradigm, to Democratic Confederalism, and the principles Equality, Gender Liberation, Ecological Life, and Democracy. We're taking part in the MSF and also participated in the Ecology Forum last January.[3] Most people are dissatisfied with the current system but don't think they have any way to change it. They

---

2   See accounts of the Mesopotamian Social Forums held in Amed, by João Romão, "Mesopotamia Social Forum (MSF) in Diyarbakir," *Transform!*, October 2009 (at transform-network.net); and Janet Biehl, "Report from the Mesopotamian Social Forum," *New Compass*, October 2011 (at new-compass.net). –trans.

3   The Ecology Forum was held January 29-30, 2011, in Amed. –trans.

have hopes and expectations, but they don't do anything to fulfill them. We don't want only to discuss—we want to take practical action! Even here at the MSF!

This house is a symbol of opposition to capitalism and the consumer society. We want to build things ourselves and be able to live from our work. Perhaps this building can become a work building, where projects can be developed and finished, or perhaps it can be used according to personal need. Our projects aren't intended only for Kurdistan— they can be built anywhere. We're knitting together a broad solidarity network—we have contacts in the Black Sea region and in Istanbul, with people who trade in tea or produce T-shirts. All over the world, people manufacture things locally by hand, and this project too can become part of an international network for such production.

What projects do you have in Wêranşar?

We have a piece of land about as big as Sümer Park.[4] Our goal is to build forty-eight houses there. To date we've built ten, which were occupied in November. They'll stand in rows of six, as a kind of six-family collective. Every family living there will have a house of 140 square meters floor space and another 90 square meters outside for a garden. We actually proposed building houses of only 90 square meters, but the families wanted at least 140. And so that's what we did. In between and around these six houses is another 450 square meters of space that could be used for a children's playground, farming, or whatever. It's up to each six-family collective what they do with their 450 square meters.

---

4   The park is about 4.5 hectares.

Who laid out the lots? Were they previously occupied?

They weren't occupied. The parcel previously belonged to the Wêranşar municipal government—it was an official green space where they wanted to erect a school, an agricultural center, or a park. We proposed building the Ax û Av Collective there, and the city donated it to us. But the families want to pay off the debt anyway—they earn money by selling the pickles and such that they produce, and they want to use their income to pay down the debt. In addition, they've offered to perform services for the city government, again to work off the debt.

The Wêranşar municipal government had wanted to establish an Ecology Academy. The Ax û Av people proposed to build the Ecology Academy themselves, also to help pay off the debt. The government accepted that proposal, and in October they're going to start construction.

How long does it take to build one of the clay houses?

It usually takes about fifteen days, but longer, if our people have to work elsewhere. When everyone participates and no one's busy with anything else, it takes fifteen days.

How much do the materials cost?

The price isn't very high, but the families involved with the cooperative in Wêranşar can't finance it easily. For the price of a typical apartment in Wêranşar, you can build ten of these houses. But for our families, the financing isn't simple. Their networks of friends donate materials. It's a collective, they practice mutual aid. We just came to Wêranşar with an idea—we're not project leaders or engineers, just guys with an idea. We've only got energy and industry to give to the project. The people there had expectations in us constructing the houses. And now we have expectations in the people, in a kind of counter-solidarity. It's a give-and-take.

Is it important that the houses look like "normal" houses, rather than clay houses, to motivate people to participate?

Unfortunately there's a modernity fever at work: people always want what's up-to-date and superficial. That happens here in Amed too, as you can see from all the new high-rises and construction sites. It happens in Paris and in every German city as well. Everywhere you see the same philosophy. We think it's destructive of nature, of both human nature and the environment. On TV and in movies, people see beautiful homes, which influences what they think they should own. So in order that the people involved in our project don't feel inferior, we've designed the houses to be somewhat similar. But they're also essentially different in that they are more beautiful, more pleasant, and especially cheaper, even when it comes to operating costs like heat.

And we aspire to democratic neighborliness. It's not that two or three families live, each on its own, next to each other. Rather, we want to make possible a communal solidarity such as you normally don't find in urban high-rises.

Initially the women didn't want to live in the clay houses because they were afraid they'd be dirty. Of course they got this fear from images of houses they saw on television. But after they got to know these houses better, their fears vanished. Not that the women alone held this view. The men also wanted to have garages, parking spots, or upper stories.

Do cooperative members have cars?

Many have motorcycles—in fact, Wêranşar is famous for its motorcycles. We're deliberately trying to keep the streets narrow so that there's no temptation to get a car. We don't want to ban cars, but cars aren't absolutely necessary. And if somehow owning a car is absolutely necessary for some purpose, then the owner can park it at a distance and use it as needed. A car is as big as a room and takes up the same amount of space. We'd rather build playgrounds. That sounds like typical mayor or city-government propaganda, but we can make better use of fields, gardens, and open spaces for the people.

Do the houses have indoor bathrooms?

When we specify that a house has to look superficially like other houses, then it has to have the normal amenities, like a toilet. The difference is that the democratic-ecological balance must be maintained—that is, construction must proceed democratically, even in procuring construction materials like tiles.

What do you mean by "democratic"?

Decisions about construction have to be made democratically. Even a six-year-old child has to be able to help decide whether something should be this way or that. We try to ensure collective and democratic participation, such as by asking children whether they like a certain house or room. That gets people more involved in the whole project.

But we've experienced a small catastrophe: those of us who came up with this idea are men, and in this highly feudal province of Wêranşar, the women said of the kitchen, "That's my place, my turf! Don't come in here!" I didn't feel I had a right to say, "No! That doesn't belong to you, it belongs to everyone. We're in on this together, and everyone participates." That's hard to say. But in the end we resolved the problem with them. It was all discussed and explained.

The forty-eight delegates of the families who comprise the cooperative are all women. Women, not men, represent the cooperative. Forty-eight families are each represented by one person, whether she's a mother, daughter, or grandmother.

Does any land or house ever become privately owned, or do they all remain communal property?

Each house and garden is considered living space for one family. It's the space where one family's life unfolds around its familiar things, a house or a garden. Everything outside the house is completely collective. The cooperative owns the land beneath the house, and the cooperative consists of all the families who live there. If a family wishes to move away, the house isn't sold to new people who want to move there—it's passed on to them.

Is everything in the cooperative, including the work, organized collectively? Does everyone receive the same wage?

After six houses in Wêranşar were finished, we offered the six families a wage to help build the other houses. But they said, "No! You didn't work for money, but you still came here, and you worked so much. Now we too want to work together without payment." It's real solidarity. But if someone who has money shows interest in building a collective, we discuss whether they should provide the materials, or even pay people the same wage and work under collective conditions.

One more thing: when products of the cooperative are sold, the money earned is collectively distributed to the families who worked on those products. Those who didn't do anything on those products don't receive any money.

Are people accepted as cooperative members only if they work?

Not all areas of life are organized in the cooperative yet, let alone in the city. We're still a work in progress, and so a few families have jobs outside. In-house production isn't sufficient to provide for everyone and to meet all needs. But if in-house production brought in enough that everyone could live on it, then probably we wouldn't need normal wage labor anymore. We live according to the possibilities of our in-house production and are as self-sufficient as possible.

To pay for medical care, people need money. Wouldn't you still have to sell products externally to get it?

The way we conceive money, people can live more or less according to their real needs and can do without luxury items. When I said that the families that don't work also don't receive anything, I didn't mean "The hell with them! They get nothing!" I meant that because they work outside, they don't need the money from the in-house production as much, and since they don't work for the collective, they don't get any of that money. It's just logical.

Someone told us that 170 people have applied to join the cooperative. Do they have to be traditional families? Or can they be groups of friends, single parents, childless people—or a couple with one or two kids who want their children to grow up with others but don't want any more of their own?

The homes reflect family relations in the surrounding area of Wêranşar, and here there are only families, with no serious differences among them. There are no singles, exceptional families, or nontraditional groups. The Ax û Av Cooperative was created to help needy families, not to finance an alternative life. It's oriented toward this population group. Of course, people who live in the city but are unemployed and poor could move here and live here. The goal is to help the needy. But if we broaden the project to the cities, maybe affluent people can build such homes there.

Do you plan to take this project further, or are you planning to stop at some point and do something else?

The Wêranşar project is now at the center of our attention, but there are also other possibilities we'd like to explore. For example, I would like to expand the tomato cultivation in Licê, so it satisfies our own needs and contributes to the local community. But at the moment we're building this project in Wêranşar, and we want to see it through to the end. We say, "We have no choice but to succeed with this project." We have to be successful. But even if we fail to bring it to completion, we will see ourselves as successful, because we dared something, we initiated something that many people regard as utopian or impossible or else they have a "wait and see" attitude. It's very important for us to put our ideas and thoughts into practice and not just talk about them.

3.2 The Economy as a Springboard for the Liberation of Women

The Kurdish freedom movement refuses to separate economics from other aspects of society. In traditional society, women are "imprisoned" in their homes and are responsible only for the work of reproduction. But through employment and their own income, they can achieve greater self-reliance and self-awareness, to the point of leaving behind their traditional roles. So that this process does not lead to excessive individualism, it's being attempted collectively, in accordance with the political project.

We interviewed members of the women's cooperative in Bağlar, a district in Amed City.

3.2.1 The Bağlar Women's Cooperative in Amed

We met in the inner courtyard of the house where the cooperative has its workshop. It's a sewing workshop with about fifteen machines. Around the table sit about ten women and their current leader, to whom we posed our questions.

How did the Bağlar Women's Cooperative emerge, and what is its relationship to the council system? Do you sit on the city council as the representative of the cooperative?

Today sixty percent of the women in the women's movement are in prison—they've been arrested. So the institutions are woefully underpopulated. I'm busy all day in the cooperative and try to supervise the tasks—no one else is available. So I don't have time to go to the council meetings. But the speaker still forwards the minutes of council meetings to me. I have a seat in the 101-member standing council.[5] And I participate in the economics committee, as the representative of the cooperative, because that committee's goal is to advance cooperatives. We also have committees made up of people who work in the cooperative.

What we do is, we go to the district councils and talk to the women there. They tell us what their problems are and how they are exploited at home. We then try to teach them about the capitalist system and explain how an alternative can be created. Then they'll say something like "I don't want to work ten hours a day, only five, because I want to have time for my children." Then we discuss how in practical terms we can build the alternative system. We explain how a cooperative functions, and the women make their own suggestions. So the council system has laid the basis by which they can develop themselves economically in the cooperatives.

For example, the local textile coop came about as a result of a discussion in which the women were saying that we needed a women's council. Based on that, we developed a better foundation for the work of the coops. You go into a district and discuss with the people. In conversation you'll get the sense of the women's talents, abilities, and wishes, and then you'll try to develop something appropriate.

Does your Bağlar coop receive outside support?

We took support from the British embassy for a project once. But usually we turn it down. One reason is that the bureaucratic procedures are

---

5   See 1.2, "The Amed City Council."

torturous. But another is that in Democratic Autonomy we're trying to create things out of our own powers and not depend on help from elsewhere.

Are the government's arrests weakening your work in the Bağlar coop?

The arrests began after the communal elections of April 14, 2009. Now there's a very intensive arrest wave, especially in Şirnex and Izmir. The people arrested are usually BDP workers, as well as mayors and officeholders and other representatives. But among women, the targets are now often activists from the women's movement, not necessarily BDP. I have the impression that the arrests are increasing, but I can't tell you any specific numbers.

What is the actual goal of the coop?

The goal is to support women, of whatever origin, economically, culturally, and socially. We do so in many different ways. To combat violence against women, for example, we collaborate with the DÖKH,[6] a federation of nine or ten different women's groups in Amed. We differ from other groups in that while they're trying to address psychological, physical, and sexual violence against women, we work primarily on economic violence. We help women create their own relations of production, where they can work and participate.

Apart from the coop work, there are situations in which a woman urgently needs paid work and has to find a job. Employment agencies exist that will place women in temporary jobs, where they'll earn about 100 lira per day. But 30 or 40 lira go to the agency, and so the

---

6   See 4.1, "The Free Democratic Women's Movement."

women receive only about half of what they've earned. So here too women's work is exploited. We're trying to change that, but it's hard because the temp agencies are supported by the state. So we've started doing job placement ourselves. A woman looking for work can go to the BDP and say, "I need work"—and they'll send the woman to us.

In addition, neighborhood unions, various institutions, employers' associations will come to us and say "We have people who are looking for work," or "We're offering work." If a doctor in the area tells us, "I need someone to take care of my children," we'll provide someone. The people who come to us know we do our work, so we can play the role of an agency.

Do you make sure it's "good" work and that the women aren't exploited?

Of course, employers sometimes exploit the women, especially in seasonal work, or if a businessman hires a woman to clean his house—that's not a public or transparent workplace. If a woman is hired as a babysitter but has to do all the housework too, she's being exploited and is also under psychological pressure. We try to intervene by talking to her about her working conditions, and then we try to talk to the employer and clarify the situation somehow. That's difficult, of course—often there's not a lot we can do. And it must be dealt with quickly. More must be done in this area, but we're doing the best we can with our limited resources.

What is production like?

When we went to the district council and spoke to the women, as I explained, it turned out that many of them had worked with textiles. They had experience and were talented. So we set up a cooperative that would not only give them work but preserve Kurdish culture: the women produce traditional clothing.

One of these days, when economic conditions permit, we want to expand our production capacity. In the meantime the women must become better educated both in practical work and in social subjects so they can take part fully. In practical terms, they're learning how to print on T-shirts. They're not professionals yet, but they're learning, and it's in motion. That might seem simple, as if it's nothing special. But for the women who are doing the producing, it's very special. Because previously they could not have imagined that they could manage anything. We're trying to bring the women out of their homes and start producing things.

How self-motivated are the women?

At one council meeting a woman assured us that she could make excellent marmalade. We talked about it but hesitated, because marmalade is already being sold in the shops—we told her we should think of something original to make. Now, traditionally many watermelons are grown in Amed. Those that aren't eaten get fed to the cows. The woman who talked about marmalade explained that she hates to dispose of the extra watermelons this way, so one day she tried making marmalade from them. "It tasted so good!" she said. "We could produce that!" We tried it, and it really did taste good. So from the surplus watermelons, we're now planning to make marmalade.

Tell us about the textile work.

Today we have nine women working in textiles. When we were first talking to women in the districts, many of the two hundred or so said they could do textile work but didn't feel ready to work professionally. So we sent them to take a course that the municipal government offers, and there they learned textile work. As I said, we want to expand our production so that many more, once they take this course, will be able to work.

113

You're going to need larger production facilities, and machines.

We talked about that yesterday. We don't have machines for textile work here, but in Amed there are some, provided by the EU, that are standing around unused. We'd like to bring them here. But mostly, as I said, we want to expand without getting help from others. Today the women work in a city-owned assembly center in Sümer Park. But they have only a small area. We're looking for a place where up to one hundred people can work. The goal is to produce not just traditional clothing but clothing that the whole region can use. So we've recently extended our working hours.

How do you market your products?

There's currently no proper market where textile products can be offered and sold. But the women's movement and the BDP have many contacts. We have many friends in this area, and when we go to weddings, or conferences, or other public events, we wear the traditional outfits we've made. People are drawn to them and want to buy them. Right now what we're producing is sufficient to cover the demand. But we're working with the district government of Bağlar on opening a women's bazaar, where women can sell things they've made themselves, like this clothing and the marmalade and so on. Only women will be able to work in the bazaar, including the security people. It's to take place every day, not just once a week.

How is the cooperative structured?

Everyone who works there participates in its decision-making processes, communally, modeled on the example of the Zapatista cooperatives. Self-critically I'd say that we've addressed this issue intensively only in the last two years—very late. Be that as it may, our organization as a coop must conform to the laws of the state. So every year we elect a seven-member board. We urge women to run for election who have not come from the women's movement or the BDP—who just work in production. But while this is a very young project, the women have little practical experience and don't dare very much. I'm on the board myself. The decisions are made collectively.

What does the coop own? For example, does the marmalade belong to the woman who produced it?

The women here have many good and creative ideas, but they don't trust themselves to function outside the home. So they come to us. To make marmalade alone is really not a cooperative effort. The women can make marmalade very well at home, but they don't get any compensation for it. But to produce something along with other women, that means very clearly that they all get something for their work.

When you say the women don't want to go outside, do you mean they don't have confidence that they can produce something for the public? Or that they don't dare go into the streets?

Both, actually. Violence against women doesn't just mean domestic violence—by a husband, father, or brother. Women also face violence in public. Some women adopt patriarchal ways of thinking and act like men, going around frightening other women. And finally it also happens on the part of the state institutions. We're always confronted with violence, so we withdraw to our homes and don't have the guts to show ourselves in public. At the women's council, many women show a woeful lack of self-confidence. They say, "I can't do anything. I can't do anything at all. I can't manage anything." Even though they do and manage everything at home, they say, "I can't do anything. What do you want from me?" Other women have enough confidence to leave

115

home but not enough to participate in a production process or achieve anything in public. Our task is to show women that they really can do things and to build up their self-confidence.

How old are the women? And are they all poor, or do some more affluent women join because they find the project interesting?

No, affluent women don't come here. And women who have a certain educational level stay away. It's mainly women from the poorer social strata who work here. They're mostly older—the youngest is thirty-six. They are mainly uneducated women who've worked at home. Many of them don't know Turkish and so couldn't get a job at a regular workplace.

To supplement school education, the women can take classes. A community center in this neighborhood offers a computer course and a musical class, on playing the erbane drum. A few women take singing lessons at the culture house, and there are also other cultural offerings. We have a focus on health issues as well, and we often have someone from the medical association, or a nurse sent by the municipal government, come to lecture. Last month we had an event on the subject of breast cancer. We have regular informational events on legal issues as well. A person from the Human Rights Association will come and lecture about women's rights. People come from the women's academy to lecture on social sexism or the "femicide" campaign.[7] They lecture and then take questions and discuss. Cultural and social work is necessary too—there are women who've lived here in Amed for thirty years and don't know what the city walls look like because they've never had the opportunity to go there. So we take them on a tour of the city, so they can see our culture's historical sites.

---

7   Deliberate murder of women because of their gender. –trans.

Who paid for the costs of the tour?

When the products of the cooperative are sold, the proceeds are first used to pay for raw materials. Then twenty-five percent of the income goes into a common fund. The rest is divided among the individual women. The common fund is there so that in the future more women can benefit form the coop's work. The cost for the bus trip to Heskîf was paid for partly from this pool and partly by the municipal government.[8] The common pool is also used for emergency cases. Recently a member of one of the women's families had to undergo surgery but didn't have enough money. The surgery was financed from this common fund. Whenever we go into the common fund for emergencies, we replenish it with income from the coop.

Can the women who work in the coop live on the income, even if they have, say, two children to raise alone?

At the Mesopotamian Social Forum, women organized the food. They established a budget. Everyone's expenses were reimbursed, and the income was distributed fairly. Not much was left over for the common fund. But that wasn't one of the ongoing kinds of work—it was a onetime thing. Maybe it will be enough to live on for one or two months, or maybe it will go for a young woman's school fees. But in the ongoing work—like the textile coop or the women's movement restaurant—enough income is generated that the women can support themselves and their families.

Does the neighborhood accept the cooperative? Do the men cause problems when they don't want their wives to be economically

---

8   Heskîf (Hasankeyf) is a historical site on the Tigris River.

independent? Or do the men, husbands, neighbors give it their support?

> The attitude of the husbands is not really positive. But we have a clear advantage in that the movement exists—even in relation to the women's question. The husbands who are tied to the movement try somehow to overcome their negative view of women. They have to work on themselves. That helps us—especially in the councils, where you'll notice men giving up their places to women.
>
> As for the neighbors, we had a problem when we first moved here. Around the corner there's a café where alcohol is served. Sometimes when the men sitting in the café look out the window, they'll see women coming and going. They annoy the women with looks or even words. We've tried to stop that by talking to the council and to the neighbors. We told them in Kurdish that we're from the movement and explained the kind of work we're doing here. Then we went to this café with someone from the council and explained it to the men there too. Since then the annoyances have been much fewer.

Has women's work in the coop affected gender roles at home?

> At first many women came here secretly, without their husbands knowing, or they had to argue in order to be allowed to come here. But over time something's changed in the society. If a woman comes home with money and says, "Look, I'm also contributing to the budget, I'm also bringing money in," then maybe it doesn't change a man's complete opinion, but it weakens some of his reservations a little. Husbands become more open to their wives going outside and working. And another fact: the stronger a woman becomes and the more self-confident she gets, then the less likely she is to allow her husband or other men to oppress her.

What is your personal motivation for working here?

I think the work in the coop is important, because I'm convinced that society can become free only when the women are free. More and more often, since the development of the Kurdish freedom struggle, women have fought on the front lines—they've become cadres and have helped direct the movement as a vanguard. That's of great importance. I'm thirty years old. Ten years ago my brother, who had studied at the university, had me under his thumb and controlled me. But since then the movement got stronger, and views changed—and now I can work here.

How are the cooperatives connected? How do they support one another?

Without maintaining a dialogue among themselves, the coops can't work in a meaningful way. All our social, cultural, and ideological work is interconnected. No one in our movement works wholly on their own. The coops work autonomously to a certain extent, but there's always exchange and interconnection. There are twelve women's cooperatives, and all belong to the women's movement—that is, they're interconnected. The DTK is the big umbrella, and under it is the economics committee I mentioned, where the coops are also represented. I've traveled to visit all the coops, and I've brought their contributions back here. They have a lively exchange going on among themselves.

Are there coops in Wan and Gewer?

In Gewer there are twenty-two communes that are coops. But they're closed to the outside and don't accept foreign journalists. They're anarchists [spoken with a smile]—they don't maintain strong connections to us but proceed with their own work. There are also coops that have detached themselves from capitalism. They don't use money as a means of exchange—they only exchange commodities. Coops exist in Şirnex, but they've not developed very far. And Wan has a women's cooperative, but the state repression has blocked its work— everyone has been arrested.

How do the projects pay full-time workers like yourself?

I was trained as an office administrator, but I don't really do that work. If I did, I could earn something. But the right jobs aren't here. I work for the coop, but I can't sew, so ethically it would be incorrect for me to claim a share of the income. The movement supports me with a small stipend. It's not enough, so I need alternative sources of income. Some friends of mine have a publishing house. I do help edit manuscripts and get a little money for that.

3.2.2   In Amed, Resmiye Can't See the Stars at Night

How rocky the road can be for individual women is illustrated by this short report on the Ekin Women's Cooperative in Wêranşar.

The Ekin Women's Coop, a café and restaurant, was founded in 2009. The city government lets the women use the beautiful eighteenth-century building rent-free—including even the costs of electricity and water. Five women and one man work in the coop; the man is the grill master. Salaries are paid with the income from the enterprise. The cooperative has a board, consisting of fifteen women with one chairperson and representatives.

Wêranşar, which has 140,000 inhabitants, was long known as "Rubble City." But the municipal government has been doing renovation work and new building projects and as a result Wêranşar has become a beautiful small city. The population is traditionally conservative, and it's not easy to do women's work here, as one of the women told us. Women are almost completely absent from the sidewalks; the few who appear wear the headscarf.

Resmiye (her name has been changed), to who we talked, is an exception: she wears jeans and sneakers and no headscarf. She complains that the BDP doesn't support women like herself enough and wishes it offered more social activities for women: "We have to get them out of their houses!"

The situation of women is much discussed in the neighborhood councils, which meet weekly. In cases of domestic violence, representatives of the neighborhood council go to the family and try to resolve the problem internally, without calling in the police. A violent husband can be sanctioned creatively: if he is employed in the municipal government, his salary can be turned over to the wife.

But the commune, Resmiye believes, should encourage women to go outside their homes and participate in social activities, and it should create more jobs for women. Women's coops, selling food and handicrafts, offer women a way to gain an income and contribute to the family support. And she believes that more young women should attend university.

Resmiye lives at home with her parents, as is usual for unmarried women. She comes from a "patriotic" family that votes BDP. Her father was tortured by the police, in an interrogation that broke his shoulder. The family originally came from a village near Wêranşar but were expelled. Once the situation eased, they returned, and now lives in a poor neighborhood of Wêranşar.

Resmiye's parents wanted a traditional life for her and insisted that she wear a headscarf. She refused, and so for two years she didn't go outside. When she also refused to wear a skirt, her father cut up her pants. She wanted to go to university, and when her parents didn't permit it, she went on a hunger strike. As she stood firm in her insistence on being able to live the life she chose, she suffered violence. The beatings from her father, she says, were more painful than the later handcuffs of the police.

At some point she said to her parents: "The life that you want for me would be my death. You might as well kill me." What finally changed the situation? we asked. "I just kept talking," she says, "and I never stopped rejecting my parents' life plan for me. Finally they understood that it was pointless to try to force me." The parents also were afraid that she would stir up discontent in their female relatives. They had reason—two cousins began to rebel too, but when their family resisted, they gave up. But Resmiye rebelled for so long that her parents yielded.

Arrested for political work, she was sentenced to two years in prison and spent eight months in Riha; she was released in November 2010. Before her arrest, she encouraged her younger sister to stand up to their parents. In her absence, the father bullied the sister. When Resmiye found out about it after her release, she threatened him: "If you do that to my sister again, I'll make sure you end up like I did!" Meaning, in prison.

But her parents had made her life miserable for so long and threatened her so much that now she wanted to turn the tables. At a certain point, both her brothers came to support her. When male acquaintances came to visit Resmiye, they didn't object, and if someone flirted with Resmiye, they joked around. They agree with Resmiye and her sister that they will have no dowry:

Our sisters are not to be sold. They're not cows. They must marry for love.

Today Resmiye is relatively independent. She can tell her family, "I'll be away next week, I have something to do in Amed," and they won't object. But she can't turn all her dreams into reality. She would like to move into one of the clay houses of the Ax û Av Cooperative, but she can't, not only because her parents don't permit it, but also because the cooperative's homes are reserved for poor families; single people can't become members.

And like so many other people involved in Kurdish civil society, Resmiye lives under the constant threat of prison. A proceeding is pending against her that could bring her a multiyear prison sentence. But she won't give up her activities. And she can't imagine living in a big city like Amed: "It's so cramped there, and you can't see the stars."

3.3 Tendencies for Absorption into the Market Economy

The projects portrayed here have a strong orientation toward noncapitalist economic relations, based on subsistence and cooperation. But if and when their families and communities become tied to the capitalist market, they will have reached a critical moment.

A much-discussed classical example is the microfinance industry, whose programs are geared especially to women, offering them a small amount of credit in order to start a trade. But since the credit—mostly with double-digit interest rates—must be paid back within a short time, the women and their families become locked in a spiral of debt, from which it's difficult to free themselves. Then, instead of going to school, the children must work to pay off the mother's debt. The intention was just the opposite. The mistake was to place the self-determination of women and their families in the hands of the market.

Solidarity projects of "fair trade" are illuminating—either they let people create a free space for self-determination or else they bring them into dependency. In a free society, the goal of the economy can only be one: self-determination. And that's always a collective question and a matter for everyone's participation.

4 | Changing Gender Relations

Democratic Confederalism aims to overthrow male domination, because it rejects all forms of domination and demands communal life. As such, Democratic Confederalism is a women's system. It is the first step for the liberation of women.

In this chapter we would like to present several projects that attempt to implement the liberation of gender, one of the pillars of Democratic Confederalism. We interviewed female members of a BDP-led municipal government, a cooperative laundry, a women's association, a women's support center, and a women's academy; we talked about their goals, conditions, difficulties, and practices. Although there are autonomous women's institutions in every area of work and life, the liberation of gender is not considered the exclusive task of the

125

women's movement. Gender liberation is also much discussed by members of ecology groups, economic projects, the academies, and the councils. For gender liberation is considered a key value in social reconstruction; the extent to which it is achieved is the extent to which the liberatory principles of Democratic Confederalism are put into practice. So movement activists scrutinize family structures and conduct campaigns against sexual violence.

Gender liberation entails a transformation of traditional gender roles for both sexes and comprises a new orientation in all social areas, and consequently intersects with other aspects of liberation work. The radical women's movement and its BDP representatives in the municipal government are at the forefront of the work on gender liberation—they called to life most of the projects we present, and the autonomous women's institutions network with them. So we will begin with a short account of the Free Democratic Women's Movement.[1]

---

1   Demokratik Özgür Kadın Hareketi, DÖKH.

4.1   The Free Democratic Women's Movement

The Free Democratic Women's Movement, DÖKH, was founded in 2003 by hundreds of Kurdish women activists, to bring together women from different social, cultural, and political backgrounds and to become an umbrella organization to fight gender inequality, racism, nationalism, militarism, sexism, environmental destruction, and economic exploitation.

Whenever men make decisions for women and go over their heads, they ignore the will of the women. That's the mentality of the state.

The DÖKH attempts to strengthen the will of women to struggle against a male-dominated system and build their own more humane system, one in which women can demand their rights and their freedom.

Democratic Confederalism means that the society is organized by women, that the society's mentality is changed, and that taboos are broken.

The founding of the women's councils was an important step toward self-empowerment. Convinced that democracy, ecology, and gender liberation represent the solution to the problems of humanity, the DÖKH struggles for gender liberation and is organized in all social strata, in order to achieve both equality and liberty.

The popular council took this declaration of women's will and incorporated it into a convention with the municipal government. So now, for example, in cases of domestic violence, the council imposes sanctions on the violent husband. This convention exists because of the women's councils and is valid in every Kurdish city and town where the BDP holds power. As in this example, the struggle for the liberation of gender is effecting tangible changes in people's lives.

4.2 Communal Projects for Women in Sûr

Sûr is the oldest and poorest neighborhood in Amed. It lies within the old city wall and is crisscrossed by small, incomprehensible alleys. The BDP has been in power here since 1999. The district's mayor, Abdullah Demirbaş, has been in office since 2004.[2]

Sûr has severe social problems. Many immigrants live here—people whose villages were destroyed, forcing them to resettle. Poverty, unemployment, drug dependency, violence against women, rape, and prostitution are widespread. Since the 2009 municipal elections, the Sûr government has had a women's department—no such thing existed previously. The BDP has pledged, regardless of whether a male or female holds the mayoralty, to maintain that department.

Gülbahar Örnek is responsible for the women's projects in the districts.[3] Three women's centers have been opened, to support women in difficult circumstances. Here is our interview with Gülbahar Örnek:

How did your work begin?

We spent the first six months going to the women in the neighborhoods of Sûr and asking them what their needs were: "What would you do

---

2   See 1.4, "The Dual Structure."

3   Gülbahar Örnek was born in 1985 in a poor neighborhood and studied agricultural engineering. In March 2007 she was elected to the Sûr municipal council and became deputy mayor. (According to the BDP's rules, if a party mayor is male, his deputy must be female.) When Sûr mayor Abdullah Demirbaş was arrested and imprisoned at the end of 2009, Örnek succeeded him: in early 2010, she became mayor of Sûr. At twenty-five, she was one of the youngest mayors in the country. –trans.

if you were mayor?" We developed our projects to conform to their answers. We established art centers and art studios, offering courses in jewelry making and handicrafts, as well as Kurdish-language courses. After a year we noticed how successful these women were and what good products they made. We made contact with sales outlets and went to various stores and said, "There are women who make pickles—you could sell them. There are women in our neighborhood who make jewelry—you could sell it. They do very good work, including custom manufacturing for individual tastes." This project was very important, because it was a way to fight poverty, and to allow women to earn their own income. The number of women who participated grew. They formed groups of about twenty, according to their individual abilities. One group pickled cucumbers, the others produced jewelry or henna. Then they made further sales at wedding halls. Finally one friend from Istanbul suggested an agency to bring together employers and women seeking work.

How many women found work that way?

The project of producing goods, and our office, began a year ago. Initially we put a lot of effort into getting women out of their homes, to become active, and to organize their time differently.

The first Office for Equality was in Bursa [in Northwestern Turkey]. "Equality" as practiced meant equality of different religious groups and ethnicities—Kurds, Turks, Armenians, and Assyrians. But for us the equality of women was also important. So when we set up the office here in Sûr, we expanded the Bursa project. It's the first office of this kind in Turkey. The Interior Ministry will probably refuse to recognize it and blame the Sûr government for setting it up in the first place—which tells you something about our problems.

What does that official recognition depend on?

The ministry has to approve the office. Since Sûr established it without prior agreement or approval, the ministry might even remove Mayor Abdullah Demirbaş from office. They did that to him once before, after which the city had to hold new elections.

Does this Office for Equality apply only to Sûr?

Yes, in Sûr most people live in great poverty. The neighborhoods of Diclekent and Kayapinar have a middle class—people there are doing better financially and can afford to hire a nanny or a house cleaner. So the Office of Equality facilitates contact between people. Now 150 women from Sûr have found employment in Diclekent or Kayapinar. Previously only five or six worked there.

Do women who clean houses or care for children receive a minimum wage? Who decides how much they are paid? How can you be sure that a third-party employment agency doesn't exploit them?

The employment agency determined the wage. But we only find the jobs for the women—they have to negotiate the wage themselves. They have the right to say, "That's not enough pay, I don't want this job, find me another one."

What other projects are under way?

Well, we had a project where women once a month went to the theater or a movie, or eat out, or take a day off. They really didn't have to do anything—our goal was actually just to get them outside the house. Then they developed their own preferences. They decided which weekday they wanted to have free, and when they wanted to work. That created *an atmosphere in which their work gained value. When we organized seminars on hygiene, on the history of women, and on workers' rights, women attended them all and stayed to the end. At the beginning our goal was to protect them from violence—when they became more independent financially, they'd be better able to resist domestic violence. But we also tried to perpetuate certain traditions: for example, in Kurdistan women customarily get together once a week to make pasta for a family. While they cook, they talk about problems in the neighborhood, such as whether someone is sick, or needs help. And now they discuss each week what issues to bring to the attention of the mayor.*

Are these discussions moderated? Does someone decide on the topics, or are soap operas and makeup also discussed?

The pasta making isn't a political discussion—it's an old Kurdish tradition that at some point was lost and that we wanted to revive. Insofar as the conversations have a leader, traditionally the oldest in the group handles it. But no one says, "Today we will talk about this topic." Instead they say, "Have you heard? X is sick." They talk about social problems, but there's no agenda. We wanted with this project to preserve a certain culture and to keep a tradition alive, so that people could mutually aid each other and develop a collectivity.

Has the Call for Democratic Autonomy had any effect on the women's' projects?

The women who join these projects without previous political experience have to be taught what Democratic Autonomy is. So we're organizing seminars to explain it to them. Our projects are tied to Democratic Autonomy, are connected to it, so the support is a two-way street. But let it not be said that every women on the street really understands what Democratic Autonomy is.

4.3   A Laundry in Sûr

Four different districts of Amed have established laundries as a matter of social policy. This laundry in Sûr, started in 2001, was the first. While the women wash and dry their clothes, their children are cared for. There's a room for children between four and five years and a morning and afternoon group, in which maybe fifteen children are cared for by a teacher, who has pedagogical training and can speak Kurdish with them. Women who are involved with other social projects or are taking classes make the most use of the child care. We interviewed two laundry workers.

You offer child care only to children aged four and five. Why did you set that limit?

> *We care for children starting at age four because at that age they can already play relatively independently.*

You speak Kurdish to these under-six children. Are you trying to teach them before the Turkish state gets hold of them?

> *We don't have anything against the preschools. Basically preschool education is a very good thing when its goal is to educate the child. Here in Kurdistan, however, the Turkish state is trying to force children to assimilate. After my training, I worked in preschool—and it's against the law to speak even one word of Kurdish to the children. A further state goal is to loosen the children's ties to their families and to replace them with ties to the state. But we don't want the children to forget their native tongue.*

Is the child care you offer free of charge?

Yes, it's free, and the all the materials are free, even the laundry detergent. In the building next door we've set up a tandoor house with seven ovens where women can bake bread. They bring the flour from home. Thanks to the Sûr government, two women are already selling their bread in shops, and so have their own income.

What hours are you open? How much is the laundry used?

We're open Monday to Friday, from eight to four. On the weekends a guard is on the premises. The house is also used as a social meeting place. In the winter we average 750 laundry visits each week, because then the weather often interrupts electrical service in people's homes, and because in the winter they usually have less money on hand and can't afford laundry detergent anymore. In summer the number of laundry visits drops to about 300 per week.

You offer a great service. Why aren't more people here now?

At the moment the washing machines are broken. We opened anyway because the house isn't used only for laundry. We work with DIKASUM, Amed's municipal center for women's affairs. The laundry facility is also a place where women can come and talk about their problems. We work directly with the women's shelter, where women can stay in time of crisis. So it's important that we keep our doors open. Now it's noon, which is a less busy time, because the women are taking care of things at home. But this morning a few women were here.

How long have the washing machines been broken, and who's responsible for fixing them?

> They've been broken for twenty days. Two are still working—we're keeping them available for the elderly. The office has been informed. But before it can award a repair contract, it has to take bids. There has to be a public request for proposals. This bureaucratic process delays the whole thing, but we at least have to make sure the elderly can do their laundry.

We're here to document the development of Democratic Autonomy. Are the people who use the laundry aware that they are participating in that process?

> They surely know. Not just because of the Call for Democratic Autonomy. Since we [the BDP] were elected to the municipal government in 1999, people have noticed changes, and they know we brought them about. Since we've been in office, more and more coops and women's projects and other grassroots efforts have developed. Democratic Autonomy has begun—these projects are its foundation stones!

4.4 A Women's Support Center in Amed

We interviewed several workers at KADEM, which is a women's support center in Amed.[4]

Tell us about your project.

> *The women's center was founded by the Amed city government. Two full-time workers are responsible for the whole house, four for the educational programs, and one teacher each for art and Kurdish. The first goal is to empower women to come out of their homes. The men in this city spend a lot of time in men's cafés. As soon as there's a problem or a fight at home, they leave the house. But women don't usually have that option. The center offers various classes, which the women can take and learn to make things and earn money.*

> *When a girl says to her mother, "Mama, buy me this toy," she once had to answer, "We'll ask your father if it's okay." Today a woman earns 350 lira just by taking the twenty-day course, after which she can produce different things. The mother can now say to the child, "Wait till I finish this class—then I'll get you the toy." It's very unusual for a woman to no longer be accountable to her husband but to decide for herself how to spend her money.*

> *The classes teach women how to produce traditional clothing, how to embroider, how to decorate tablecloths and other linens with sequins, and then how to sell these things. In another class women can learn*

---

4   Kadın Destek Merkezi, KADEM.

how to play the traditional erbane drum, not only as a instrument but as a social activity. They can organize a musical group to play the drums together and so are no longer just housewives.

We've realized that women who previously knew nothing but housework are often very interested in art. At our center they can take part in art projects like marbleizing paper, then exhibit their work. We also offer literacy courses. Formerly women had no identification papers of their own and so could not even go to school. Many reach the age of forty without being able to read or write. Our course was developed for them.

After the Call for Democratic Autonomy, we started teaching the literacy class in Kurdish, so women can learn to read and write not only in Turkish but in their native tongue. And at home they can teach their children to speak, read, and write Kurdish. We realized that the women learn much faster in the Kurdish literacy classes. Many women said, "I can't attend the class because I don't have anyone to look after the children," so we now offer child care. We set up a Child Development Room where, during the class, trained people care for children aged three to six. The caregivers all speak Kurdish with these kindergarten children—it's important. For girls over fifteen, we offer classes where they can earn a certificate that allows them to attend school. We offer our classes in two shifts, morning and afternoon. Those who go to school in the morning can take our classes in the afternoon and vice versa.

Many immigrants from Mêrdîn and Êlih live here in Sûr, forced to resettle after the destruction of their villages. Often they don't have identification papers, which were either lost or burned. Many were hiding for political reasons and officially didn't exist. Now, when these people acquire identification, they often choose to avoid government institutions on principle. For example, a full-time employee here was forcibly resettled. She attended school only up to the third grade, and her sister didn't attend school at all. Even after they obtained ID papers, they were furious at the system and refused to attend a government school. Here we offer such girls an alternative, a way to use their time meaningfully.

We also offer textile classes, where women can learn techniques and become proficient enough to work in a textile factory. We've seen this happen in recent years with ten women. Before they attended the class, they were housewives; now they're employed.

We also offer social counseling. If a woman has experienced violence at home, or has other kinds of problems, we can put her in contact with a lawyer or a psychologist or place her in the city's women's shelter. We offer a class on law, where women can learn their rights. At first they just listen, but soon they begin to understand, and finally they apply what they've learned. One woman learned to say to her husband, "Stop. Don't come one step further. Here is your boundary. I have rights, as I learned at Kadem." Before, such women thought everything that happened to them was correct and that they had no rights.

How were your classes initially received?

At first some women were doubtful and wondered, "Can I really attend this class" or "What will my husband think?" They came to class secretly—and if someone in the family needed them, they rushed home. This initial period was difficult, but we worked through it, because we all tried to solve the problems together. For our classes, we don't just passively wait for applications to come in. We go directly to the families, or speak with people on the street, and offer them the classes.

How is Kadem financed? Does the city government pay for it?

Since it was established by the municipal women's department, Sûr covers the costs. It pays the salaries of the two full-timers, the rent, and the course materials. It also finances the four employees who come from the popular education houses. The Kurdish teacher is paid for by Kurdî-Der.[5]

Do some women have a problem with your connection to the government, because they identify with different politics?

We accept women with other political opinions besides ours. But often a funny thing happens. Let's say Fatma doesn't talk to her neighbor Ayçe because she has a different political opinion. Then they both come to the class and start talking. They decide that the political difference is not so big after all, and both recognize that the prejudices against us Kurds are stirred up by the ruling class.

Why are only a few women present here today?

At the moment it's summer vacation, when we don't offer any classes. The women you see here have just applied for the next class. In summertime many of the women who live in the city go back to the villages to help with farm work.

---

5   See 6.7, "The Kurdî-Der Language Center in Amed."

The women who take classes, acquire skills, and become financially independent—are they aware that they are part of the process of Democratic Autonomy?

> *They know that the transformation has begun, a transitional phase from one system to another. Not everyone has a clear awareness of what the new system will look like. We offer seminars on Democratic Autonomy, and we talk about it in our classes and studios and also the kindergartens, because assimilation begins with education. The state requires children to enter preschool at age five, where they learn only Turkish and forget their native tongue. It's important to us to offer alternatives, because only through them can Democratic Autonomy become comprehensible.*

4.5   The Binevş Women's Counseling Center

Turkey has no multidisciplinary women's counseling centers, only specialized ones like health centers. But Kurdish municipalities where the BDP is in power are now developing multidisciplinary centers.

We interviewed several employees and supporters of the Binevş Women's Counseling Center in Colemêrg.[6] The conversation could not be recorded for security reasons. So we offer here a summary of the discussion, based on our notes.

The idea for the counseling center came from the deputy mayor, and it was founded with her support. The Colemêrg city government finances the center and pays the salaries of its employees. It was supposed to open in January 2011, but due to harassment by security forces it was not until the end of september the employees could begin with their work. Many people who are active in the city government have been arrested in recent months.[7] Obviously the counseling center is under surveillance. The state evidently finds it inconvenient for women to become aware of their rights.

The center hasn't yet started work on specific projects. Currently its staff is taking an inventory, asking the local women about their interests and needs. Based on those results, they'll develop projects.

A few sociologists work at the center on a volunteer basis—they help women with legal, health, and psychological problems. First they assess a women's need for help, then refer her to the appropriate specialist. But the center is still under construction, and more specialists must still be found.

The center values confidentiality. Only a few advisers know the details of their clients' situations. That's important in order to guarantee

---

6   Binevş Kadın Danışma Merkezi.
7   See 1.4, "The Dual Structure."

protection and prevent future problems. The fact that the women sought help at the counseling center is not mentioned, since feudal society condemns seeking outside help for a problem. "Why didn't you talk about it with me, so that we could solve it?" the men will ask. "Why do you have to broadcast its existence?"

Women in Colemêrg province have a notably higher status than women elsewhere—they experience less violence, and honor killings are excluded. But sexual violence is still too common. Discussion of the subject is taboo, and women have no public institutions to which they can turn. Even though the woman is the victim, she is blamed and punished for being "polluted." Such women suffer years of psychological consequences, including sexual and other marital problems, and also problems with their children.

In its education work, the counseling center is planning to focus on health, family planning, the rights of women, and human rights in general. The health classes will offer information about breast cancer and on children's illnesses. Because so many people here can't read or write, it will run literacy classes. It will also hold classes for men and husbands. A male sociologist will teach seminars for men on sexuality, family planning, and contraception. Women won't be able to attend— it'd be uncomfortable for them if they later met these men on the street.

The women's center works with the councils and sends a representative to the Colemêrg women's council.[8] It also maintains contacts with other NGOs, for example KESK, the umbrella union for civil servants.[9] It hasn't yet set up an educational program on Democratic Autonomy, but its members understand that the concept must be brought to life. "We already live in an autonomous province," said one. "That's our reality."

---

8   See 1.3.3, "The Colemêrg Women's Council."

9   Kamu Emekçileri Sendikaları Konfederasyonu.

4.6   Female Activists and Their Families

When we interviewed members of the Amed Women's Academy,[10] we asked them how much their families supported them as activist.

You've said the women's movement is a large family. Do women activists have to break with their own families, or do the families accept them and their work?

Many of us come from families that are closely tied to the Kurdish freedom movement, patriotic families. Mostly they respect our work. Frankly, we're in a state of war and grew up in the resistance. A large part of the society is politicized. So many people are open-minded about women organizing, at least to a certain extent. I learned from my mother how to behave at a meeting and how to organize people.

For our part, we like the family as an institution about as much as we like the state. The state creates things in its own likeness, and the traditional family is one of them. The state reproduces its hierarchical structure in the family. That's true for both traditional and modern families. The family of our aspirations, by contrast, is one that's open to a democratization process. We're not talking about democratic families, because right now that would raise expectations too high.

Kurdish families aren't yet really open to the new system, Democratic Autonomy. They haven't yet internalized it. We, the activists, have very much internalized it, and it's our responsibility to make change,

---

10   See 6.3, "The Amed Women's Academy."

to impart ideas of Democratic Autonomy to families, even if it's only in small steps. We can start talking about it at home the way we do outside. When our families see how seriously we take it, that will affect them. Of course, discussions are often very difficult. Doors get slammed, people shout. But a lot of perseverance and discussion has also begun to create change in families.

But to get back to your question: we're not for severing all ties with the family. We're for bringing families into this process and then bringing the process to fruition along with them. Separating oneself from the family is tantamount to ending all one's relationships, to alienating oneself even from oneself. So as we construct democracy, we need to bring our families along.

What happens with women who are free and self-reliant but also want to have children? In Germany that's an important subject—how to reconcile work and family.

We don't consider family and work to be all that much in contradiction. Here women who are married and have children are also active. But some movement women dedicate themselves to the political struggle and choose not to create a family. They don't get married, they don't have children, because they regard the family as a reflection of the state and the present system, while we want to build a new, alternative society.

What about women who have children and want to become active? And women who are active now but would like to have children? Are they demanding more public child care?

A woman wanted to attend a class we were offering, but she had a child for whom she could not find care on weekends. So she thought *she couldn't take the class. We told her to bring the child along. So for two days before the class, we organized child care, so that it wouldn't be an problem. We also had a kindergarten attached to Selis Women's Counseling Center, where the women could leave their children during the daytime.[11] It's about to close, so we're organizing another one.*

Women who want to become active aren't required to leave their families and children behind, or to stay childless. There's also no law that forbids us to have relationships with men. I have a relationship with a man and nonetheless work in the women's movement. I'm trying to conduct my relationship free of traditional gender relations. We reject the position of women in the ruling patriarchal social order. If we're going to change society, then of course men and children have to be involved.

---

11 Selis Kadın Danışmanlık Merkezi is a women's counseling center in Amed. –trans.

5 | Social Ecological Transformation

Capitalism is making inroads into Kurdistan, accompanied by its systemic destruction of nature. Neoliberalism has not penetrated fully into North Kurdistan, and many people still live in close connection with nature. But projects in energy, mining, infrastructure, and agriculture, as well as war and urbanization, are damaging the environment. The military burns forests and contaminates whole swaths of land by using chemical weapons. Industrial production (as at the oil fields in Êlih), the construction of dams on the rivers, big new fossil-fuel power stations, and the growth of cities (aggravated by the forced resettlement of war refugees) all lead to the pollution of soil, air, and water and so are endangering health.

The problem can't be solved by only one environmental association, or by addressing only one aspect or one project. We must work out a perspective for the whole region and undertake a thoroughgoing transformation of society along ecological lines. In its Call for Democratic Autonomy, the DTK laid out the paradigm of a democratic, ecological and gender-liberatory society and set as goals an "ethical transformation" and an "ecological approach."

In this context, protests against environmentally destructive projects acquire great meaning, such as against increasing urbanization and massive dam projects. The dams that are now being constructed destroy important ecosystems, drive out hundreds of thousands of people, and—as in the case of the planned Ilisu Dam—flood millennia-old historical sites. In January 2011, the Mesopotamian Ecology Movement was founded to create a network of existing environmental organizations and initiatives against social-ecological destruction, in order to strengthen sometimes-marginal protests and to promote the construction of an ecological society.

In this chapter we will look at the ecology movement and its environmental organizations, their goals, their focal points, and their main projects.

5.1   The Mesopotamian Ecology Movement

Many Kurds live according to sustainable patters out of sheer necessity—they can't afford out-of-control consumption. But if in the future they live in harmony with nature as a matter of their own free will, it will in part be due to the efforts of the Mesopotamian Ecology Movement. It considers energy policy, economic questions, and long-term raising of consciousness to be just as important as resistance to specific energy-technical megaprojects.

At the moment the movement is still in its infancy. We interviewed activists in Amed in 2011.

What is the Mesopotamian Ecology Movement?

It's a brand-new organization, stemming from the Ecology Forum held in January 2011 and discussions at the second Mesopotamian Social Forum in September 2011. We've been discussing the ecological perspectives that should be implemented in Turkey and Kurdistan. But to date people have organized only locally and have not joined together. There are also areas where activists are entirely lacking. In general we're missing wide-scale organization. At the Ecology Forum, we decided to create a general organization. We drafted a constitution and a program, which we sent to all these local groups. Now we're trying to work on practical goals and raise ecological awareness in the general population.

How do ecological problems affect people's daily lives and the economy?

The biggest problems are in the cities. In the villages, ecological lifeways are ninety percent in place. Capitalist modernity hasn't yet penetrated into rural areas, although that's changing. But in ecological terms, the cities are the problem zones. We should not increase our energy use—we should reduce it. Meanwhile we must develop not only an awareness of the need for saving energy, but also a new ecological orientation, by which we can reconstruct the cities along ecological lines. Today Kurdish cities are industrializing, according to the well-known capitalist template. But their growth and their traffic must be limited. So we have to work in the towns, to introduce planning measures that enhance local public transportation rather than car traffic. The discrepancy between town and country must be diminished. Foodstuffs consumed in the cities should come from the surrounding areas as much as possible. And we must reject genetically modified produce—it shouldn't be cultivated at all.

Why are there so many environmental activists in the Black Sea region?

Many destructive projects are under way there. The rivers and streams are being dammed, and the mountainous areas are being destroyed by mines. Almost everywhere in the region, people are protesting, even coming out against the proposed nuclear power plant in Sinop. These protests are especially strong because the Chernobyl catastrophe in 1986 sent a lot of radioactive fallout there. And in the 1970s the left was very strong, and people today can still relate to that.

What do you think about nuclear power? What energy sources would be appropriate for the Kurdish areas and for all of Turkey? Who should make this decision?

We're opposed to nuclear power. As for renewable energy, we think it's important that the people agree to it and that it be organized in a decentralist manner. After all, solar and wind energy can become objects of corporate interest. We mustn't let control over energy generation slip from our fingers into the clutches of corporations. We think the participation and consent of residents and users is hugely important.

How much renewable energy is being generated in this region?

We haven't developed it very far yet. We're calling for new institutions to address the problem. We need a decentralized energy system with modern, effective technology, one that's not controlled by the corporations.

That will be difficult—it has to be financed.

Yes, but the problem isn't specific to his region—it's a general problem and is being discussed internationally. What's most pressing for us right now is opposing the dam projects. They'll bring us nothing but social and ecological destruction. The resistance has to come especially from the people who are directly affected.

Think of Hasankeyf, in the Tigris valley, which is to be flooded. It's not enough for two or three urban intellectuals to oppose it. The local residents must become active. Unfortunately to date, they have not sufficiently resisted. If we can't bring them around to our side, then the state and the enterprises involved will exploit that fact. They'll say, "What do you want? The people aren't against this project."

So blocking these destructive projects is our most pressing problem at the moment. Recently the guerrillas have led several actions against dams, and they've been more direct and effective than the protests by the local population. Such actions don't take place very often, but when they do, it's a way of criticizing the urban activists for not doing enough to oppose the projects.

Turkey, a country prone to earthquakes, is planning to build nuclear power plants. Is the state propagandizing nuclear power as a "bridge technology" or as a "lesser evil"? Is it pitting antinuclear and antidam activists against each other?

The ecological initiatives in the Kurdish areas reject both nuclear power and this kind of dam project equally. But unfortunately a few antinuclear groups in Turkey see hydropower as a good alternative to fossil fuels. In any case, we have less and less to celebrate. Last year antinuclear and antidam activists held a large joint demonstration in Istanbul. No one in Kurdistan defends nuclear power plants. At the moment it's not such a pressing subject because none are under construction. But Mesopotamian environmental activists are resolutely against them.

We're convinced that the transformation of people's consciousness is very important over the long term. We have to explain to people that everyone should produce less waste. We have to address the problem at its roots and make it so that people damage nature less. We don't want to consume as much energy as people in western Europe. The Turkish government is promoting the capitalist growth model, but we're trying to copy it as little as possible. It's not our development model. We have refrigerators at home and electrical lights, but we don't need much more.

What other ecological issues are you working on now?

The Kurdish freedom movement has recently worked out the theoretical foundations for an ecological society. A few decades ago Kurdish society was, by present-day standards, very ecological in practice. To a great extent, it still is. The rural people don't commit serious ecological damage. A city like Amed of course commits much more. But essentially the destruction comes from the state and its projects.

People who behave ecologically do so not because they're ecologically conscious, but because they don't have the means to destroy nature through consumer behavior. The state and the big corporations are trying to exploit nature, with projects that will lead to massive environmental destruction. In addition to the dams, pipelines for natural gas and oil passing through Kurdistan are on the agenda. The multinational mining company Rio Tinto wants to dig for gold in Dêrsim province, using potassium cyanide. Against all these projects we want to carry out stronger actions soon and help found local initiatives. We want to improve teaching about ecology in communal education centers. Ecology is now being taught in all the movement academies. Along with resisting specific projects, it's important to raise consciousness—we work on both levels.

5.2   Current Environmental Activism

Ercan Ayboga of the Initiative to Save Hasankeyf described for us the new ecological institutions in North Kurdistan—councils and associations and the Mesopotamian Ecology Movement:

We got the idea of building ecology councils during discussions in the Mesopotamian Ecology Movement. The city and provincial assemblies, that is the councils, have an ecology working area. But not all the assemblies have established committees or working groups on that subject. The councils' goal should be to bring together all the groups and institutions that have to do with ecology: the associations; the municipal environment, green space, and planning departments; and the professional organizations, especially the Architects and Engineers Professional Association.

The larger cities don't have that many associations yet, perhaps one or two. Here in Amed we have the Union of Environmental Volunteers, founded ten years ago. It worked on the Ilisu dam and did biodiversity experiments, but it's no longer active. Now a new association has emerged in Amed, but I'm not that familiar with it. Êlih has a Union of Environmental Volunteers that also fights the Ilisu dam, which is to be built nearby, and that addresses problems of air pollution. The local oil industry causes pollution and makes people sick. The plants are located very near the city. Formerly about 10,000 people worked there, but now only about 2,500. Since the Second World War, Êlih has grown from a village to a large city with about 400,000 [officially 325,000] inhabitants.

In Mêrdîn there's an association that tries to address the subject of urbanization. Here urbanization is leading to big problems, worsening the air, soil, and water quality, the way it did in 1960s and 1970s in Europe. The association emerged in reaction to environmental pollution—a few people said they couldn't just stand by and watch it happen.

In Dêrsim there are activists who work to protect the Munzur valley ecosystem. They mainly oppose dams but also pollution in the river valleys. Regional tourism is growing in Dêrsim, and some parts of the river are very polluted, because half the visitors simply throw their trash out the window. So actions have been carried out in which fifty people went into the valley, picked up the trash, and issued a statement. They're trying to get the city government involved. The state-run institutions are doing nothing, because the polluted areas lie outside the city.

The Cilo-Der Nature Association in Colemêrg has been around for six years. Cilo is the name of the tallest mountain in that province. The association works on dams. And it works on forest destruction—the military deliberately and systematically sets forest fires [in order to expose the guerrillas' hiding places] in Colemêrg, Şirnex, and Dêrsim.

In Wan there's an association that fights the pollution of Lake Wan and does educational work. Associations are emerging in the small cities, like Şirnex, which has a group that works on ecological issues. Their number is growing around the region, but they're relatively small, sometimes depending on only one or two people. If they leave, everything collapses. Of course the members work voluntarily.

Isolated groups can hardly hope to achieve real successes. When the Ecology Forum founded the Mesopotamian Ecology Movement in

January 2011, it intended to build a much-needed network. They still need more people—groups and individual activists—to dedicate themselves to creating the network in North Kurdistan.

The city governments should also be brought in. Recently some have said groups and associations alone should carry the network. But the activists finally decided to involve the municipalities, to help achieve the goals. And if they're excluded, they might not take the issue or the demands seriously. People have criticized municipal governments as institutions that aren't always interested in the grassroots, and they point to political forces within them that want to be elected and are willing to pursue entirely different interests. But since most of the city governments here are held by the BDP, the network decided to seek their participation.

5.3 "We can't just stand by!": Protesting State Energy Policy

In reaction to environmental pollution and to state energy policy, many initiatives have sprung up to unite a critique of capitalism with ecological practice. We interviewed several ecology activists.

What issues are people here concerned about?

> *There are several important ones, but the dams get people the angriest. They're causing the most destruction. Damming a river basically destroys it, and even smaller hydropower works dry them out. Fossil fuel plants—natural gas, coal, and oil—are being built near cities and villages, with catastrophic effects on people's health and the local ecology. These power plants produce most of the area's energy. And in several places mining companies are digging for coal, gold, chromium, and copper, leading to all sorts of problems. There are stone quarries in Dêrsim. At Lake Wan there's a plan to mine uranium, valued at perhaps eight billion euros. BP and Shell are active in Êlih. Shell is also conducting soil tests and drill probes around Amed.*

Are mineral reserves more of a curse than a blessing?

> *Capitalism has no pity and exploits nature without scruple. There's not much oil in North Kurdistan, except in Êlih and perhaps a few other places—at least that's what we've been told. Most of the oil is in South Kurdistan [Iraq]. It brings a lot of profit, but it also harms the environment and destroys natural areas. We're not the ones who consider oil to be wealth—it's capitalism that does. So we should focus*

our criticism on capitalism. We would all be satisfied around here—but everyone else seems interested in the scarce elements, and wants to exploit our raw materials. If the international defenders of nature and the environmental organizations don't concern themselves with this region, it will fall into the hands of the capitalists.

Do you get support from international organizations like Greenpeace?

Because of the war, Greenpeace doesn't work in this region anymore. In Ankara, ecological organizations have had discussions with Greenpeace, but in the war areas it's hard to mount big campaigns. Also on the issue of dams, Greenpeace behaves rather cautiously.

How should the energy sector be transformed? What are the top priorities?

The government says energy demand is growing at a rate of seven to eight percent annually. But the energy losses are considerable. The transmission lines lose twenty to twenty-three percent of the electricity because they're old and are seldom repaired, and because they carry so much of the electricity across long distances from east to west.

The first priority should be to overhaul the old power plants. Two billion euros are expected to be spent on the Ilisu dam, but with that money we could get two or three times more energy in other ways. The first step is to stop the dams—then we'll see whether energy demand really grows. In the meantime we can talk about where development could go.

The Turkish government says, "We consume per capita only twenty-five to thirty percent of the electricity that central and western Europe consume, so we have pent-up demand." But we shouldn't consume as much here as they do in Europe. Turkey is the state that, since the 1992 Rio summit, has had the highest increase in greenhouse gas emissions—in that twenty years, they've risen by one hundred percent. At the world climate conference in Copenhagen in December 2009, Turkey announced that it planned to counter climate change by building ever more hydropower plants. By 2030, it plans to meet thirty percent of its electricity demand from renewable energy sources. But already today twenty-five percent is met by hydropower.

What is your thinking about other forms of renewable energy?

There are a few model wind turbines in Izmir. Turkey has a lot of potential for wind power, and a law governing all renewable energy is being discussed. The EU is demanding it, but the government has been dragging its heels for a year. Some information has already leaked, and it turns out not to be what we hoped for, and will not have great state financial support.

5.4   The Cilo-Der Nature Association in Colemêrg

Kurdish culture is closely tied to nature. A Cilo-Der employee told us:

She is our second mother. Whenever we were driven away, we always took refuge in the mountains, in nature.

Said a member of the Mesopotamian Culture Center:

The Kurds talk to the mountains. Nature is for us mother, comrade, life, homeland, roof, and place of refuge.

According to another Cilo-Der employee:

In 1993 the Kurdish villages were forcibly emptied and the people were driven out. This city is really just a big village. The people brought along their rural mentality and their animals. It was beautiful there, and it's very beautiful here. But for the municipal government it's a problem that the people live here as if it were a village. And yet through urbanization they have been separated from nature and natural lifeways.

And Aysel Doğan[1] explained:

People must live in harmony with nature, because we're part of the ecological system. Why should people set themselves up against nature? But if people—individuals, entrepreneurs, states—exploit nature for their own one-sided purposes, that's a problem. Then we have to spread

---

1   See 5.6, "Green Visions: Toward an Ecological Society," and 6.4, "The Alevi Academy for Belief and Culture."

consciousness among people, through organization. They have to be
fully educated about the consequences of the destruction of nature.

We interviewed two members of the Cilo-Der Nature Association in Colemêrg about the need for action, educational work, and ecological perspectives. The association, named after Cilo Mountain, has thirty-two members and was founded in 2004.

What are the goals of Cilo-Der?

> *Our main goal is to protect nature, but we also want to raise*
> *awareness among the people so that they live more consciously in*
> *relation to nature, so that they honor nature. Cilo-Der's goal is to deal*
> *with everything that has to do with ecology and create alternatives:*
> *alternative energy, and alternative lifeways that are more connected to*
> *nature, so that people live with more ecological awareness. People here*
> *already live more or less in accord with nature. But we have to make*
> *them conscious of it and warn them of the different way of life that's*
> *on the horizon. Our philosophical outlook commit us to protecting*
> *threatened species. Everywhere in the world, even in Turkish law,*
> *the hunting of mountain goats is forbidden. But Village Guards and*
> *soldiers go into the mountains and hunt rare species in the wild in*
> *order to eat them. They don't care about species protection. We're*
> *trying to protect the animals by raising popular awareness and helping*
> *people feel closer to our natural wealth.*

Given war and repression, how can you build a stronger awareness of nature? How does Cilo-Der work with the city council and with the municipal government?

> *We go to the villages and talk to people. We want to bring ecological*
> *issues more into the councils, because it's a matter of the future.*

We've worked with the municipal government on green spaces, the water supply, trash removal, and similar things. Recently there haven't been any meetings, and we haven't yet really established a collaboration with the city council. Because of the war, people have trouble concentrating on their own work. They continually have to cope with arrests, skirmishes, and deaths. It's all part of daily life. It's hard to implement communal environmental protection since neither the councils nor the NGOs have any money. The Turkish state doesn't give us support—on the contrary, it hinders our ability to get help from abroad, such as for constructing a water treatment plant. It stipulates that the interior ministry has to approve it. That means the municipalities can't act autonomously.

How does war damage nature?

This war has been going on for thirty years now, and in numerous battles chemical weapons have been deployed. This region, the river valley of the Great Zab, has a wealth of flora and fauna. Colemêrg alone is home to about 6,500 species of plants. Moreover, the region has a significant cultural and natural history—the Assyrians and Chaldean Christians who lived here 250 or 300 years ago planted walnut and mulberry trees. The glaciers on the peaks are 20,000 to 50,000 years old. And some rare species of plants are threatened with extinction and need protection. Because of the war, plants can't grow well in the Cilo Mountain anymore—they die off and the soil is barren. We don't know exactly why, but we can see the plants dying. Also local crop yields are down. There were once many birds here, but not so many anymore, which could be because of chemical weapons or because of the noise of battle. We've also noticed that after these attacks the number of miscarriages and cancer illnesses rapidly goes up.

We've heard about forest fires set by the military.

That's right. Forty percent of the forested lands in Şemzînan and Şirnex have been denuded by arson. And special forces of the Turkish army use grenades or dynamite to catch fish in the Zab River. And all the strategic points on Turkey's borders with Iran and Iraq have been mined.

How difficult is it to recruit volunteers for ecology work?

It's the hardest thing of all. Our association has members and activists who are academics, doctors, students, and other educated people. We also try to attract people from the women's and youth movements. We assume that youth and women will be more effective than so-called academics. The people of the Middle East have an entirely different way of life from Europeans. Although we're very poor, our dining tables have abundant food—we even throw food out. Nature has been so generous to us that we're too spoiled to do anything for nature in return. We consume and live without considering the consequences. The Kurdish areas, it must be emphasized, possess great natural wealth. For centuries, imperialist powers have invaded and conquered us—they knew of our wealth; we were the ones who didn't know about it. We're the poor children of a rich country—perhaps you can understand that.

How do you educate people?

We distribute magazines that give information about environmental pollution. And we've developed brochures for schools that explain about environmental protection. We're in contact with the municipal government and with the schools and have worked on developing educational standards. Environmental education is not part of the regular school curriculum, which is devised centrally in Ankara. They don't consider regional problems, except as seen through political-ideological lenses.

Do you get support from abroad?

We're getting aid from a German foundation for our educational work. We're part of a nature defense project for Mesopotamia, the region between the Tigris and Euphrates, that's trying to block the dams. The project is pretty small, but it's important for the whole region, not only for Turkey but also for Iraq and Syria. It's of international interest, because everyone in the region depends on the water supply. Also the political academies offer ecological education.

What kind of ecological education?

About the relationship between humanity and nature, and between people and ecology. We talk about nature and environmental destruction and about the ecology movement and its demands.

So it's less about practical implementation of alternative ecological concepts?

Actually one of our goals is to make a revolution in the mentality of humanity, to sensitize them to the subject, to do a kind of consciousness formation. We're trying to raise consciousness, for example, in the city government, where we hold the mayoralty, so it can implement it in its work.

And do they?

We criticize those responsible when they make decisions that aren't ecologically acceptable. We try to influence decisions, by emphasizing the ecological aspects of an issue. We teach in the academies and invite people to report on their practical experiences.

5.5   Resistance Pickles and Other Rare Things

Another employee of the Cilo-Der Nature Association welcomed us to his home on the outskirts of Colemêrg. In the front room we found several women sitting at fifteen weaving frames and knotting carpets. Their leader was our host, and the women are employees in a project that gives them a way to earn income; it is supported financially by a Swiss association.

The wool for the carpets is dyed in the house. Organic dyestuffs are made from plants grown in the garden or from roots, leaves, and herbs foraged nearby. The project leader has studied vegetable dyes and dyeing techniques over the years, after the complex knowledge of his grandmother was lost. He has been documenting his experiences.

Nearby he maintains a small collection of seeds, especially from plants threatened with extinction and rare species from the region. He regularly goes to the river valley and collects small shoots, which he then cultivates in this garden, for example, a small kind of grape called *murek* (bird-grape). When they're a little bigger, he distributes them in the neighborhood. Many of the seeds that he showed us come from native plants. Some of them grow on the banks of the Tigris, so if the Ilisu dam is built and the river floods, they will disappear.

His collection includes not only plants that can be used for dyeing but also species of fruits and vegetables, herbs, flowers, and medicinal plants that only grow here. Among them is the "giant cucumber." This cucumber can only grow in clean water, as our host discovered after running tests with both clean and polluted water. "Capitalism will not prevail over this pickle!" he said. We baptized it the resistance pickle.

In a conversation with another environmental activist, we learned that elsewhere in Kurdistan too, individuals are trying to protect rare species by collecting seeds and distributing them. "There's a great consciousness here. In Amed and in Dêrsim I've met several people who've said it's important to protect and use the traditional, local, original seeds." Some in the Kurdish movement are discussing the establishment of a seed bank.

Many plants are being threatened with extinction, since the state is promoting the use of genetically engineered seeds. An employee of the Cilo-Der Nature Association reports:

The agricultural authorities advise the people that they should buy genetically modified seeds. They are deliberately pushing a poverty politics: by urging genetically modified seeds, they create dependency, because people have to buy the seeds every year. The problem is, ecological seeds produce only three to six kilograms of yield, but genetically modified seeds produce many times more. So it's hard for us to persuade people not to use them. We try to educate people not to produce, buy, or sell anything genetically manipulated and to use only organic farming methods. Tomorrow you should go to the market, if you have time, and get some of our famous red tomatoes. They're organically grown! Organic farming is being done in many places. The university in Dêrsim offers a course in it.

If nothing genetically manipulated were being imported or sold, this region would be pretty ecological. I'm a farmer who grows cucumbers, tomatoes, melons, and onions. Unfortunately capitalism is trying to monopolize the seeds, by destroying traditional organic farming and replacing it with its own patented gene-seeds. But it gets worse. They're patenting discoveries in nature and so claiming, by a capitalist logic of value, to own them exclusively. One example is the plant ters lale.[2] It's now been patented by a western Turkish firm even though it's a product of nature in this area.

---

2   The *ters lale*—the Crown Imperial (*Fritillaria imperialis*)—is a very old kind of lily. We were told that it's being illegally traded, bringing in US$20 to $50 per plant. Formerly, in Kurdistan, a whole sack cost about ten Turkish lira, or about $5.

5.6   Green Visions: Toward an Ecological Society

Aysel Doğan believes that the cooperatives are crucial to the creation of an ecological transformation of society.[3]

People, by their nature, reap what they sow. Nature respects all work of all lifestyles. When balance is present, humanity and nature benefit together. Society must be made aware of this fact.

The best way to create an ecological system is to build cooperatives. One of my greatest dreams is to see the construction of youth and women's villages. They could become models for the ecological system that we're aspiring to. They could provide work for hundreds of unemployed youth. Young people are hungry, and I don't mean only for nutrition—they're hungry in spiritual and psychic ways, and they lack future prospects. If young people and women work in a village cooperative, they won't be exploited and will be paid for their work. A communal life among young people can become exemplary for the whole society.

That's not so unrealistic. Cooperatives can be started in existing villages, or people who fled to the cities can return to their destroyed villages and rebuild. There are hundreds of such villages. The people can't just move back, though—they need material support. It might seem difficult, but it's not impossible. With effort and commitment, a village could be rebuilt. But we will need time too.

---

3   Aysel Doğan is an ecology activist who tries to stop the military from setting forest fires. She is the president of the Alevi Academy for Belief and Culture in Dêrsim. A few days after our interviews, she was arrested. In October 2012 she was sentenced to eighteen years in prison.

Besides these material aspects, the state causes problems. Soldiers are everywhere and behave menacingly when an empty village is resettled. In recent years people who returned to their villages were bullied and their villages were razed all over again.

The species diversity of North Kurdistan is breathtaking, but it's threatened, by the construction of new dams like Ilisu. The Great Zab Valley has many springs, rare native animal and plant species, and especially birds. Migratory birds return from their winter quarters and build their nests here. The local people call the Great Zab Valley a paradise for birds and also a water paradise. It could attract ecotourists and become an open-air university for ornithologists. In such way the mountain landscape in Colemêrg province could be protected over the long term and preserved from economic destruction. A volunteer from the nature association describes such a plan for postwar times:

The geography of this region is very special. The mountain landscape rises to 4,116 meters (13,500 feet), and because of that altitude and the glacier atop it, it's always relatively clear and cool, even during the hottest days of summer. It's never warmer than 20°C (68°F). While other Middle Eastern countries are burning up, we enjoy natural fecundity, pleasant weather, and the landscape. It might sound like an exaggeration, but this place is really paradisiacal. Maybe the people don't realize it, but the imperialists and the powerful do. That's why they are waging war here and fighting for this region.

Spring, summer, fall, and winter—they're all happening here simultaneously. Look around, and you'll see many plants growing in all four seasons. I'm thrilled by how many plants and how much nature this place offers. It has great potential for tourism. Mountain climbing alone could attract many people—we could build a gondola. Imagine an international tourist center here. But the tourism mustn't destroy nature—it must respect it, so that nothing is damaged. There shouldn't be big hotels, but nature hotels.

Countless people have passed through this region for centuries. We want people here to feel responsible for these things in the name of humanity. I want to emphasize especially the religious diversity of Colemêrg province—until the last years of the Ottoman Empire, Kurds lived here together with other peoples and religions, like Assyrians or Armenians. My grandfather for example is a Nestorian.[4] The message is that we can all live together. We're not turned in on ourselves here— we're open to everyone.

---

4 An adherent of Nestorianism, a Christian doctrine dating back to the fifth century.

6 | Education for a New Society

When a new society is being constructed, its builders must disseminate new values.

A patriarchal and feudal mentality has shaped consciousness and behavior in North Kurdistan for thousands of years and is reproduced by the existing system. How can it be broken? How can we instill grassroots democracy, ecology, and gender liberation as values of an entire society and integrate them into everyday life?

Today grassroots democracy is spreading in the area thanks to the construction of councils, and gender liberation is growing due to the struggles of the women's movement. But a deeper transformation requires a conscious mobilization of the whole society. In the Kurdish context, where access to education is not routine, education plays an enormous role. It's not a matter of earning diplomas or other certification but developing a substantive engagement with life today and appreciating the necessity of building a free, sustainable society.

Therefore construction of Democratic Autonomy rests partly on the new popular councils but also partly on the academies, which drive the Kurdish freedom movement's educational work. These academies originated in Amed in 2005, then spread to Wan, Istanbul, Izmir, Mêrdîn, Cizîr, Riha, and Mersin. There are now thirteen of them, with various foci, including nine general academies, two women's academies, and two religious academies, one for Alevis and one for Islamic beliefs. We spoke to activists from the General Political Academies in Amed and Wan, the Women's Academy in Amed, and the Alevi Academy for Belief and Culture in Dêrsim.

We spoke to representatives of other kinds of schools as well: the Mesopotamian Culture Center, which is active mainly in music and dance; the Center for Kurdish-language Education, or Kurdî-Der; and Educational Support Houses, which are for young people.

6.1   The Amed General Political Academy

We interviewed a representative of the Amed General Political Academy.

First, before we get to your academy, we'd like to know about the religious academies. Are they intended for religious people who are involved in the Kurdish freedom movement? Do they teach theology?

> *One task they perform is to analyze religion and clarify how, from a materialistic point of view, the Kurds became Muslims. The other task is to engage with basic religious questions, like what Sufism is or what the Bible says. The academies are open to the general public. The religious academies don't teach the Islamic ideology of the ruling class but rather the heart of Islam, its basic ethical teachings, its social role. Frankly, Turkey's rulers exploit the Kurdish people's religious feelings and use Islam as an instrument of rule.*

Do the academies give any thought to developing an Islamic liberation theology, like the Christian liberation theology that was developed in Latin America?

> *Abdullah Öcalan's ideas about Islam are the underpinnings for the teachings of the Alevi academy. These schools want to work out the essence of Islam and connect to the oppositional Islamic movements, which reject rulers and an Islamic state but nonetheless are connected to Islam. Examples are the resistance against the Umayyad dynasty, and Mansur al-Hallaj, who sought the essence of Islam and then was*

skinned by the Islamic rulers.[1] Other names of interest are Pir Sultan Abdal, Abu Muslim Khorasani, Babak Khorramdin, Imam Azam, Imam al-Shafi'i.

What do the political academies teach?

We teach social history: society before the state, society after the emergence of the state, slaveholder society, feudal society, capitalism, and globalization. We try to consider this history from a distinct perspective.

We also teach the history of Kurdistan. Who are the Kurds, where did they come from, what struggles have they waged, and how do they relate to other peoples of the Middle East?

Then we talk about capitalism: what it is, where it comes from, and how it became the dominant society. What role do nation-states play, and what is the origin and function of nationalism? Once we have had all these discussions, we come to the question of what society we wish to have and build.

How long does the course of study last, and who takes part in it?

The academies offer a variety of courses. First there's a three-month course—that's the one that the cadres who are to build the new society take. Then there's a one-month course, which is taken by practically everyone in the movement—in the NGOs, the BDP, the DTK, the unions, and so on. And then there's the popular education program, available to the general public, which takes place on certain weekdays,

---

1   Mansur al-Hallaj (857-922) was a Persian Sufi who was executed as a heretic. –trans.

in a conference hall, in various yards, or even in the middle of the street. Depending on demand, we offer all these educational possibilities.

After the three-month course, all participants reflect on what they have learned and formulate a critique of state and ruling class. And they do a self-criticism, which means they reflect on their personality in relation to this mentality.

In all three educational programs—one-month, three-month, and popular courses—we teach the following things: Stay away from nationalism. Stay away from scientific knowledge that has been warped by domination, the science that produces weapons, the cancerous science that's responsible for the destruction of nature. Stay away from religion that's been warped by domination and has become an instrument of the powerful. Stay away from sexism. We come into the world as women or men, and then certain roles are attributed to us. But if you want to be in this movement, if you want to build this society with us, you have to cut yourself loose from the traditional gender roles and relations.

Do you discuss homophobia and homosexuality?

Yes, we talk about that too. We don't want homosexuals to be excluded from society. On the other hand, we are opposed to people selling their bodies, making them into commodities, into a business for their livelihood.

Are you talking about prostitution?

Yes. Living out your understanding of sexuality is different from using it as a source of income. Our critique calls it the lowest form of capitalism, when you make your body into a commodity.

But there are social reasons why this occupation is the only one available to them.

Of course that reality exists, and we can't close our eyes to it. But it's something that capitalism has created, it derives from capitalism. It can be overcome.

The students surely have very different educational backgrounds. Are your various courses appropriate to all those levels?

The curriculums aren't very theoretical. A mother who never learned to read or write can, by the end, draw conclusions that are much closer to reality than those, say, of an aloof academic. Life experience is important. And for all the work of the academy, we are teachers as well as students. Our educational policy doesn't categorize participants as to whether they can read or write or whether they've got university degrees. We'll all build the new society together—illiterates, workers, and academics.

Who are the teachers?

They're usually longtime activists in the Kurdish freedom movement, who are deeply engaged with the ideology, who have analyzed various social systems and especially the movement's history and development.

Do the cadres decide who the teachers will be? Or can anyone step forward and say, "I want to be a teacher"?

In each area there are perhaps one or two dozen people who are intensively engaged with the subject. They decide among themselves who will teach which subject when. For certain fields, like philosophy, economics, and political theory, we sometimes bring in people from *outside. But for the ideological subjects, we mostly use people who come from the movement and are engaged theoretically and practically with the ideology.*

We understand that in Democratic Autonomy, the popular councils are the decision-making structures. And since the hegemonic Turkish educational system doesn't teach much about liberation, the academies are responsible for spreading knowledge and theory. But who decides who gets which education when?

The leadership of the academies decide, in consultation with the city council, when popular education will be held and which courses will be offered.

What do the grassroots think of the education here? It's offered for free.

Unfortunately Kurds don't value education all that highly. They fight well, they can wage a resistance, but they don't really like education so much.

What does that mean specifically?

We've not yet reached the goal that we set out to achieve. Over time interest has grown, but with our current cadre capacity, we can't meet the demand, because the cadres as well as the academies are targets of state repression. And we can't maintain continuity in the education of cadres because they're arrested so often. Before my group, there were two others that led the academies. They were arrested in the anti-KCK operation. Yesterday the academy in Izmir was raided, and the leadership was arrested.

How many educational units are offered in a year? With how many students?

The one-month course has between 20 and 35 students. Sometimes two courses run simultaneously. When enrollment is less than twenty, the course is canceled. When there are more than 40, two courses run concurrently. There are four to eight courses per year. And then there's the popular education. Each year 250 to 300 people attend those units. When you add on the popular education, then total enrollment rises to 5,000. Every weekend there is an educational session attended by as many as 300 people.

How are the courses publicized? How do you get students?

We'll go into the neighborhood, and ten people will come to the first class. Word gets around, and twice as many come. And next session, it increases threefold. By the end of the unit, the number is even higher.

So there's no publicity, besides going to the people and talking to them?

We're going today into this neighborhood and teaching a unit about Democratic Autonomy. The residents are interested because the education is being offered by the movement that's waging the resistance, the resistance that their children are entering. They want to understand its politics.

Where do the academies teach?

They have their own buildings. Popular education takes place inside the academies as well as outdoors, depending on the demand.

What's the minimum age for attendance?

There's no age limit. Children don't come, but youth do. Freedom, the freedom struggle, is an important subject of discussion. The people who have the most restrictions on their freedom are women, so more women come every time.

Because they're more interested, or because they have more spare time than men due to their economic situation?

It's got nothing to do with economics. The women in the Kurdish freedom movement are very well organized, so they come to the educational sessions. Among the youth, we have a problem: Kurdistan is still a colony, and the colonized psyche is such that people see themselves as less valuable than the colonizers and model themselves on the colonizers. I went through the Turkish education system, and the young people like this Western education system very much as a foundation, and they see their own education system as less valuable.

How do you foresee the work of the academies developing?

The academies are subject to repression. They have no legal status. If they had freedom, they could play the same role in the Middle East that the academies of Socrates and Plato played in ancient Greece.

Perhaps an international exchange would be possible?

I hope so. If that happened, I'd be thrilled to have made a small contribution.

6.2   The Wan General Political Academy

We interviewed an employee of the Wan General Political Academy.

When and how were the academies founded?

The Kurdish movement intended to have academies for a long time. Finally we went through a paradigm shift and developed an alternative ideology, which demanded a rethinking. All our knowledge rests basically on the European social sciences. But we criticize European social science—it's hegemonic and popularizes power.

It's a difficult task to build a system outside the state. The state is five thousand years old. It's formed people's perceptions and mentality. So when you're building a system outside the state, you have to train people to think in a new way. If you don't, then you won't succeed in detaching yourself from state-generated ideas.

Here in the Middle East dogmatic thinking is common, and critical questioning is not. But we critique European thinking as well as the religious-dogmatic thinking of the Middle East. We try to reconsider the social sciences as well as the state and democracy. We define everything anew.

We criticize the European definition of democracy. People talk about democracy, but whose? Do existing democracies really represent the interests of the people? We also consider critically Eurocentric ways of thinking. Europe thinks everything progressive had its origins there, but not every advance came from Europe. We think the Middle East also possesses deep-rooted knowledge, and we're trying to uncover it.

We want to revive the Renaissance/Reformation of the fourteenth century here in the Middle East.

What is the curriculum in the political general academy?

First we talk about the importance of education, because here in the Middle East not many are educated—education doesn't have high status here. We're trying to create a sensitivity for the importance of learning. A further point is philosophy, because the first mythologies and religious dogmas, as well as the first approaches to positivism, were developed here in the Middle East. By "Middle East," we don't just mean Kurdistan but the whole Middle East with all its various peoples. We emphasize the importance of education, and then we try to impart the spirit of inquiry, of study and testing. Because people in the Middle East believe in fate—they assume everything is predetermined and they live according to this destiny and don't look at cause and effect.

So we teach them the various philosophical tendencies of past and present. Then we teach them social and cultural history. We reject history written by the powerful. Our goal is to teach unwritten history. Slaves rose up in many rebellions, but their history has never been written. Roman history talks only about the Caesars—and much less about Spartacus. And the historical writings of the ruling class do not consider women. They're not even seen. So we try to uncover and teach the history of those about whom little or nothing has been written.

Marx is very important to us—we take him and Engels seriously. Marx wrote a good analysis of Europe in his time, although it's incomplete. We are writing the incomplete parts, and as we do so, we reinterpret Marx. We teach the history of women and the essence of social sexism. We analyze capitalist modernity and can relate especially to social scientists who opposed the system. We try to convey the history of the Middle East, of Europe, and of Kurdistan. We introduce Democratic Autonomy by asking what it is, how one would live in a society based on Democratic Autonomy, how one can live without a state. Even quantum physics is important for us, and for a while we were teaching microphysics. Above all, we try to strengthen dissident views in our cadres.

What is your main criticism of Marx?

We're critical of his analysis of domination and the state—he saw the state as progressive and necessary. But societies can exist without the state. And since Marx analyzed historical development only in terms of classes, we're also critical of that. History isn't only the history of classes—human history is actually much older. The history of class society is only five thousand years old. So you can't consider history exclusively through the lens of class. As societies developed, the means of production played a role, but not the main role. Marx analyzed the question of women's liberation only through the lens of class struggle, but we don't regard that as satisfactory. The question of women's liberation is much more far-reaching and comprehensive.

What does education have to say about collective ownership?

Let me be clear, we're not saying we've found the right solution. But we think the system that we're trying to develop comes closer than any to a right solution. Much as westerners tried, before the Renaissance, to search out the values of the ancient Greeks, we try to today to discover the old values of oriental societies. Communal society remains present in the societies of the east. Even if the capitalist system has entered the eastern societies and is developing an unbalanced way of life here, communal ways of living and thinking persist. Cities are a problem, because the cities are the center of capitalist modernity. They foster individualism and self-interestedness. So it's important to transform consciousness here, and we're trying to do that with the academies. Our goal is to bring the Kurds who've emigrated to the cities back to the communal system, but we have for the cities at the moment no solution.

What is the purpose of self-reflection and self-criticism at the end of the educational courses?

The purpose is to recognize and break one's own arrogance. During reflection, a man analyzes his ways of thinking about women, how he thinks about them and how he interacts with them. Whether he becomes cadre, whether he can become part of the work, depends on his attitudes about women. If he thinks about them regressively, that's strongly criticized and not accepted.

6.3 The Amed Women's Academy

We talked to two employees of the Amed Women's Academy.

Women's academies are an entirely new project. What work do they perform? What role do they play in the construction of Democratic Autonomy?

> *The women's academy here in Amed has existed for about a year. Women's academies are indeed new. They do research and science, conduct education, and hold workshops and study groups. In the future they could become the educational sites for Democratic Autonomy. The academies also transcribe Kurdistan's extensive oral history and archive it. The sources are very scattered. We work with women from the university—next week we're going to discuss with some of them whether and how we can work on a female writing of history.*

Where are women's academies located?

> *At present there's one here in Amed and one in Silopî, in Şirnex province. Another is being built in Wan. We all stay in contact and work toward the same goals. Our academy here in Amed is located in the Sûr district. Sûr stands out from the other districts in Amed because of its social composition and its problems. State repression is deeply felt here, especially as it affects children, youth, and women. We organize activities with women who live in the district. Some of them don't leave their homes, so we visit them at home in order to get to know them and gain their trust. Once they trust us, they can make their way to the academies. In society generally, relationships are getting colder and people are ever more isolated, all of which*

makes home visits very important. So they're our first task. We listen to people's problems and write reports about them, which gives us a basis to find solutions, one step at a time.

What principles guide your work?

We have in mind a political vision in which women play a vanguard role. The liberation of women, and of gender, is as significant as the liberation of men in society. In fact, the liberation of woman is a liberation of the whole society. It's no simple matter to achieve it—we face many difficulties, including sometimes with our own comrades.

We teach that the Neolithic, when farming and animal husbandry began, was also the beginning of history, and society was organized matricentrically. For the longest period of human history, society was organized matricentrically. Only in the last five thousand years has patriarchy shaped society. But these five thousand years have drilled patriarchy so deeply into the minds of people that it's very difficult even to grasp this concept.

How many women take part in the educational courses? Do you educate female cadres and employees of initiatives, NGOs, and parties? How often do the courses take place?

They usually consist of 15 to 30 people. We offer ten-day courses, one-month courses, and two- or three-month courses. They're organized and planned by the groups that are here at the time. We set them up to be as interactive as possible, so we can really have a discussion. We don't want the classical teacher-student relationship. Recently we ran two of the three-month courses with about fifteen young women. Here they talked about history from women's perspective. We really delved deep, formulated analyses, and then tried to draw personal and social conclusions.

We conduct popular education in the framework of popular assemblies, especially in the neighborhoods. The women talk about their problems, and we try to work out solutions. Recently at a meeting in Sûr, sixty women took part! For us that's more important than the educational programs, because conversations about their problems are like therapy for the women. And we gain their trust. If in the future they want to attend educational events, they'll be ready. On November 25, 2010, the International Day for the Elimination of Violence Against Women, there were in Amed many lecture forums on this subject. We led a discussion where women could describe their daily problems at home—it went pretty well. The academy is represented in the city council and the district councils and works with them.

Do the women's academies offer education for men?

Most of the courses are for women only, especially the longer ones, and we don't offer any for men only. But a month after the academy opened in Sûr, we held a mixed course for both sexes, with representatives of institutions and NGOs, on the subject of social sexism.

Coeducation is a new area for us. The level is honestly very high, and we get into many discussions and arguments. It's important and beneficial to discuss certain subjects with men. But our overriding purpose is to raise consciousness among women. Our longer-term units are aimed at them.

Do you have discussions about women in other countries, like Clara Zetkin and Alexandra Kollontai?

We consider Rosa Luxemburg and Alexandra Kollontai to be our forerunners as freedom fighters, and we try to do right by their legacy. We're working now on preparing a literature list, and here we are open to your suggestions. *We also publish a quarterly magazine, and in the last two issues we profiled international Kurdish women activists and personalities, like Leyla Qasim.[2] Unfortunately, in historical revolutions, the women who took part were not valued highly and stayed in the background. We're determined to research their history, revive their stories, and place them in the foreground.*

Who teaches at the women's academy?

We aren't academics. We're active in other institutions too. For example, I work at the women's academy and also at the women's cooperative. The women's movement is a very big family, consisting of many institutions. Some concern themselves explicitly with violence against women, while others work for women's economic independence and try to create employment possibilities. All these institutions are part of the Kurdish freedom movement.

---

2   Leyla Qasim (1952-74) was an Iraqi Kurd who spoke out against the Ba'ath regime. As a student at Baghdad University, she was accused of plotting to assassinate Saddam Hussein. She was arrested, tortured, and executed. –trans.

6.4   The Alevi Academy for Belief and Culture

We interviewed Aysel Doğan, the head of the Alevi Academy for Belief and Culture, located in Dêrsim.

Can you tell us about the academy?

Any one person may have several identities. You have ethnic and religious identities, and if you're politically active, you also have a political identity. But the Turkish state, in denial of this fact, says everyone who lives here is Turkish and Sunni, that is Islamic. But we object, saying, "No, we're not Turks, we're Kurds. And no, we're not Sunnis, but Alevis." In order to make the state hear our voices, we have to struggle, and so we struggle.

The state's mentality of denial manifests in the assimilation policy, which we consider cultural genocide. The state doesn't recognize Alevism. It says, "There's no such thing. You're a Muslim." Then later it says, "Okay, you're Alevi, but that's ... such-and-such." And it defines Alevism according to its own conceptions. While the state plays with your religious identity, you unconsciously begin to absorb its preconceptions. Next thing you know, you're defining yourself as a Muslim. Alevism has to be defended against this state policy. We regard ourselves as Qizilbash Alevis. We're trying to defend the cultural and philosophical uniqueness of Alevism against the state's "Alevi policy."

We're an academy, but our work isn't really scientific. We grapple with questions like "Where do I come from?" and "Why am I this way?" There's a university that researches the origins of Alevism—supposedly. And what conclusions do they reach? They attribute its origins to Central

Asia, or they tie it to Haji Bektash Veli or to Jalal ad-Din Rumi.[3] And so ultimately they tie it to Muhammad. But my roots are not to be found in this person. And it's also not your job to research my roots.

Fethullah Gülen, who is trying to spread a version of Sunni Islam here, creates confusion about Alevism. The Gülen movement even organizes among the Alevis. Gülen asks you, "Who are you?" and you're confused, and you try to define yourself. And he says, "No, you're wrong. You're not this, you're that." Moreover, the movement has a lot of money. It gives people work, and it sends their children to school for free or it grants student scholarships. In these ways Gülen tries to Islamicize Qizilbash Alevism.

To this we say that we're not the Alevis that they are defining. Qizilbash Alevism has for example no tradition of cem houses [ceremonial buildings]. Our holy places are mountains and stones and waters. We have the pirs [Alevi clerics], but otherwise no dogma. Qizilbash Alevism has its own system with its own rules. Maybe in the modern sense it's not possible to have a free and egalitarian religion, but unlike other religious societies, we have democratic forms of organization.

The state of course wants to destroy this. That's why it's squeezing us. And it's playing another little game with Alevism. In the cem house, the semah [a mystical dance ritual of the Alevis] is performed, and the governor or the army comes to watch. There's nothing like that in our tradition. All our holy places are being flooded by the dams. They say, "If your places were really sacred, then we'd be punished." But the sacredness of the Munzur River applies to us and not to them. They

---

3   Haji Bektash Veli (1209-71) and Jalal ad-Din Rumi (1207-73) were both thirteenth-century Muslim mystics. Rumi, a Persian, is well known in the West as a poet. –trans.

say, "You say the Munzur is sacred. Well, we've dammed the Munzur, and it can't do anything to us!"

They've begun to exploit our holy places commercially. For example, the mountain Düzgün Baba ("Father Düzgün") is holy to us. We go there, pray, kiss the stones, light candles, dance semah, kill a sacrificial animal, and then leave. But slowly the state is penetrating there. It's forcing its rules on us. It's planted its informers there and pays the salary of some of the pirs. So not much remains of Alevism there. We're resisting as best we can.

Do you have regular meetings? Or are there educational forums? Do you go to families and talk to them?

We don't go from house to house like missionaries. The people in this community are Alevis anyway. We write press statements, hold discussion forums, and meet with the pirs. When religious people come here, we talk to them. We help them perform rituals in the holy places. We maintain the pathways to the holy places. Or we organize places for them to stay overnight, if they need it. We try to protect the religious places.

Since the holy places are endangered by the dams, the state sent a so-called scientist here who's supposed to provide expert opinion. He says that there are only stones here and no indication that it is a holy place. But these stones are sacred for us. We protect the places that he reviewed—we've built walls around them. For me every stone, to which we light candles, is sacred. But you can't explain that to a scientist. For him, there has to be a mosque standing there or a church or some other building—otherwise he'll say the place isn't holy. Look at Düzgün Baba—it's a mountain. Zel is the place of a goddess. For me they're sacred. That's why we work to protect them.

How did you get the idea for the academy? When did it open?

We opened it a year ago. A few friends got together, elected our executive, and went to the state authorities and told them we were going to defend Alevism against them. We drew up statutes that we showed them. Our constitution is broad—the association encompasses women's activities, youth, and nature protection. We founded an association that's part of Democratic Autonomy. The Alevis are organized here. We don't want to depend on getting support from outside. We're building something through our own efforts, something we can pass on to the next generations who can continue the work. At the same time, the Alevis here can educate themselves further. If the state asks, "Who are you?" or "What are Alevis?" the people will be able to answer.

Do pirs come here and work with you? And are the premises also used for the cem or other ceremonies?

Interestingly, the pirs are being assimilated faster than others. They work at the university or the cem houses and get money from the state. Semah is danced there every Thursday. But that's not common here— we dance semah only at the Hizir fast. We've tried to win the pirs away from the state. But one of them is ruled by fear, and the other has an employment problem. They don't earn any money from us, so they go to the state and become civil servants. We don't recognize these pirs. They're not our pirs, but those of the state. But other pirs do come here. With them we organize discussion forums and dance semah.

We wanted to build a small house for the academy, but it would have cost too much. We have this place thanks to financial support from Kurds in Europe, but it's really too small. One day we're going to buy a piece of land and build a house. Maybe not tomorrow, but the day after tomorrow.

You were in prison for ten years, during which time much changed. When you came out two years ago, people were organized very differently—not centrally anymore, but base-democratically. What do you think of that? Were you surprised?

It wasn't surprising for me because I stayed informed. It doesn't matter how isolated you are: when you're twenty years old and active in a movement, you know what's going on. We followed the developments on TV, or if there was no TV, we read about them in the paper. And if there was no paper, visitors told us. Anyone who hoped that the movement would develop in a different way would have been surprised. But it would have been much more of a surprise if there had been no development at all.

I was in the mountains for only a short time; otherwise I worked always among the people, so I expected this development. But Dêrsim has gone backward. In the 1990s Dêrsim was much better off—then the state forced fifty percent of the people to migrate. It gave the people who stayed on only one option: "Adjust yourself and be polite." What could they do? They could pretend to conform, while rejecting the state even more bitterly. But this attitude is a great obstacle. If you can say that the state is a murderer only behind its back, then you can't speak freely—that's repression.

In the 1990s this region was much more radical. The people were much more opposed to the state. When they were driven from their villages, they also lost their acceptance of the state. I planted trees in my village; today soldiers probably sit under these trees. There are fewer military strongpoints here today, than when I was in these mountains in 1991 and 1992. At that time there were far more barracks and outposts. That's why the Gülen movement is here now. That's very bad. Once upon a time we didn't hear Islamic prayers being spoken aloud. But today, when they give alms to poor people, they read them the Fatiha or some other sura.

When I came out of prison, I could not have said that Dêrsim had developed much further. But when a community come to understand what the state is and that it massacres our people and denies our identity, then we can be silent for only so long. Finally we'll be ready to stand up for our rights and to fight. And so I don't lose hope!

6.5   Educational Support Houses in Wan

In 2002, city governments where the pro-Kurdish party had taken power began building Educational Support Houses.[4] The one in Wan was built in 2008. In the first year only volunteers worked there, but since 2009 the teachers can be employed, and more such houses have been built in several neighborhoods.

We met with a group of ten teachers, all males, age thirty and over. They welcomed us warmly, showed us the classrooms, and explained their work.

How many women teach here, and what's the proportion of female students?

All together eighteen teachers work here, of whom three are women. They teach history and physics. And one of the executive board members is a woman. Seventy percent of our students are girls. The Kurdish freedom movement now has a paradigm for gender liberation, enjoining the people, "Send your daughter to the university!" Since that began, the orientation of the people in the province is much improved. We set ourselves the goal of having at least forty percent of the positions occupied by women, but we got too few applications. That's probably because women have better university degrees, and so they're more employable by the state, which pays betters salaries than we can.

---

4   Eğitim Destek Evi.

How old are your students?

We teach young people seventeen to twenty-one. If the students want to pass the universities' entrance exams, they prepare by going to expensive private schools. But children from poor families usually can't afford it, and Islamic sects revise the lessons in favor of [the government's] assimilation policy. We don't want the children to be strangers to their own culture. We teach the main general subjects, and we also offer two hours a week of Kurdish-language instruction. We'd like to teach all the subjects in Kurdish. We teach nine classes in two groups, we have weekend courses for the eleventh and twelfth grades, and we offer courses during the week for students with high school diplomas. We're only closed on Mondays.

Last year this school was raided. Five volunteer teachers were arrested. Two of them have since been released, but three remain imprisoned. And we expect further repression. The three imprisoned ones still haven't been charged, even though they're in custody. Teachers are being criminalized at least in part because of their membership in Eğitim-Sen, the education union—it's an oppositional force and the driving force behind the construction of Educational Support Houses like this one. The raid took place at around four in the morning. They took all the computers. At that time of night no one was here, so they broke down the doors. Over the phone we later learned that the teachers of the union had been invited to a meeting. In a telephone conversation that was bugged, someone said, "Please bring me two eggs." The police had interpreted this to be two Molotov cocktails.

In the Turkish educational system, everything is taught frontally in rows. Do you use alternative methods?

We'd love to do that, but we're preparing young people for the university admissions exams, and so we have a time problem: we *have to teach them the material of four years of high school in one year. Beyond that, we were all educated in the old system, and it's difficult to put aside old habits. For ten years there's been talk, in Turkey, about changing the education system, but it hasn't happened.*

Not since the founding of the Turkish republic, eighty years ago, has the education system really been good. The teaching language is exclusively Turkish, and at the daily flag ceremony, the students are forced to swear the oath that says, among other things, "Happy is he who can call himself a Turk!" We want to counter the assimilation policy and teach in Kurdish. Our students think in Kurdish, but they have to verbalize in Turkish. If they're going to be successful in school, they have to be taught in their native tongue. Turkish students have it easier and are more successful because they're taught in their native tongue.

How do you compensate for this linguistic disadvantage?

There's a lot of repression against Kurdish-language instruction. In 2004 the Kurdî-Der was founded, because the students wanted Kurdish instruction not only in private but in the schools. [Prime Minister] Erdoğan, during his visit to Germany in 2008, came out against assimilation there and for obligatory native-tongue teaching. So then people here demonstrated for Kurdish instruction in the schools. Erdoğan's response: "Whoever demands that, wants to divide the country." By that logic Erdoğan wants to divide Germany!

When I was in school, I got angry with my mother. She told me I should only speak Turkish. Then at the university we recognized that we were different; we discovered alternatives and fought back. After two years I was expelled, but I could still take the exam. I'm Alevi, but the only religion that was taught was Sunni Islam. We're in an impossible situation. We feel ashamed that we can't speak our native tongue. And then we're laughed at because our Turkish isn't that good.

How many students do you teach in one year?

In 2010, four hundred students signed up—the demand had doubled. Across Turkey we in the Educational Support Houses taught thirteen thousand students. Our goal is to give still more students this possibility.

Who finances the houses?

The students don't have to pay anything. The municipal governments pay the rent and the teachers' salaries. Our teacher pay is lower than that in the state-run schools. But then, the 1968 revolutionaries taught the people entirely uncompensated, so we also want to do that. We reject teaching at a state-run school. We have students who are much poorer than we are, and for them we collect money. We work with different associations, like the Peace Mothers,[5] and the Association for Prisoners Support.[6] They refer us to students from particularly needy families.

What are the house's decision-making structures?

We have weekly and monthly meetings, where we discuss everything and try to come to consensus decisions. Only when we can't come to an agreement do we vote. Every class has two representatives, one

---

5   See 1.6.1, "The Peace Mothers."

6   See 1.6.3, "The Association for Prisoners Support."

male and one female student. They take part in the meetings and have a vote. They can formulate critiques of the teachers. Moreover we have various committees: for literature, language, technology, and for the school regulations. We don't have a secretary, but we all feel responsible for those tasks. We have no director that gives us orders, but a coordinator. We make all decisions together according to the council principle.

6.6   Mesopotamian Culture Center in Colemêrg

The goal of the Mesopotamian Culture Center is to advance and protect the richly diverse Kurdish culture. Kurdish culture is currently exposed to a genocide, according to an employee of the culture center. Writers are banned, and between 1913 and 1925 thousands of books were burned and are now lost forever. Many poets were forbidden to write, and if they dared to write anyway, they were arrested. "If our writings weren't banned, we'd have full libraries," said one of the employees who talked to us about the culture center.

Kurdish culture and history survive especially because of oral transmission, through song and dance. The culture center's archive consists of oral transmission, and culture is preserved through the people. Eighty percent of the singers are mothers, and in the songs they express their pain. In Colemêrg alone, 280 different dances are known, and the gowend dance is particularly important. "They express our lives," one person told us, "which are shaped by war but also by joy and culture."

A few European films are based on Kurdish tales, but much has been destroyed or otherwise lost. Only now are the songs of the dengbêj being researched and documented.[7] The older women in the villages, are asked about their stories, and the stories are written down. "This truth is important for us—they have suffered much pain and preserved our history." In the villages there's sometimes no electricity, so the villagers can rely on technology only part of the time. Publications should be made and also an archive of documentary movies should be set up.

---

7   Dengbêj is traditional Kurdish speak-singing. For more information, see Constanze Letsch, "Silenced Kurdish Storytellers Sing Again," *Guardian*, December 28, 2011. –trans.

Kurdish culture is tied to nature. You can see the connection in the many flower patterns on the clothing. "We can say of the Kurdish language: the Kurds talk to the mountains. Nature is our mother, comrade, live, homeland, roof, and place of refuge." "We Kurds are very emotional," an interviewee told us. "We were never for conflict and war, we're for peace, but we also have the right to resist, which we do especially with songs and texts, not physically."

In Turkey today, thirty-eight Mesopotamian culture centers have been built, employing two hundred artists. The center in Colemêrg is named after the poet Feqiyê Teyran, who described this region's history almost five hundred years ago in his ballads. [8] He had to go into exile because of a war. The center has a large hall and five rooms for its activities. It is open all day, every day. Two days a week it offers guitar instruction, two other days theater workshops and instruction in dengbêj. The offerings are announced by word of mouth, but also through flyers and public forums. The center also offers courses in history, language, painting, and music. Most in demand are classes on the dengbêj speak-singing and on gowend dance.

---

8   Feqiyê Teyran (1590-1660) was a Kurdish classical poet and fabulist. –trans.

6.7   The Kurdî-Der Language Center in Amed

We interviewed two employees of the Kurdî-Der Language Center. They wrote this introduction themselves, discussing the practical work of the association more than the principles of Democratic Autonomy, but the two are inseparable: "Politics is hiding even in the water that we drink."

The Association for Research and Development of the Kurdish Language, or Kurdî-Der, was founded in 2006. The headquarters is in Amed. We have twenty-six offices around Turkey: in Izmir, Mersin, Adana, and of course in the Kurdish areas. Since the founding of the Turkish republic, the Kurdish language has been suppressed. The republic's philosophy is to assimilate all the peoples of Anatolia, to "Turkify" them. But the areas of present-day Turkey have long been home to many peoples. The republic has assimilated or denied them, through the education system and the repression of their language, or through physical annihilation, like the massacres of the Greek people in September 1956. Around 20 million Kurds live in the Turkish part of Kurdistan, but because of the Turkish state's philosophy, they aren't recognized.

In the first years after the founding of the republic, people who spoke Kurdish were criminalized and persecuted. Still today in the state-run institutions, no Kurdish may be spoken, and Kurdish schoolchildren may not be taught in their native tongue. To outsiders it may seem that the use of Kurdish language is no longer generally punished, and that the situation of the Kurds has improved, but it's not so. To take one of countless examples, the newspapers reported about a woman in Izmir who went to a doctor and spoke Kurdish.

She wasn't treated—she was humiliated and sent away. In Konya in 2008 young people from Amed talked to their relatives on the telephone in Kurdish. They were arrested for "disturbing the peace." In the state-run institutions people are not helped unless they speak Turkish, and the civil servant who lets them speak anything else will experience consequences.

Linguistically, Kurdish and Turkish are two fundamentally different languages. Kurdish has letters that don't exist in Turkish, like Q, W, and X. Even if Turkish officials say that people are free to speak the Kurdish language today, the 1928 law is still in effect that criminalizes the use of these letters. It's called "Law for the Protection of the Turkish Alphabet."

The state's view of the Kurdish language is connected to the Kurdish question as a whole. Turkish television programs from private broadcasters like Show TV or Fox TV use these letters. They're used in the touristic strongholds in the west. But for the Kurds themselves they are still forbidden. A double standard is applied.

Because the Kurdish language is banned from the education system, we fear that in the future it will go extinct. We founded Kurdî-Der to research the language, to develop it further, and to teach people their native tongue. But one association alone can't teach a population of 20 million. The people who come to us to study neglect other things, because the classes take place after work or after school, in their free time. And we're allowed to teach only members of the association. According to the Association Law, only people of legal age can be members. Even though language is learned best in childhood and adolescence, we're only permitted to teach adults. And we can send teachers to groups that want to open an association themselves.

Kurdî-Der receives no state support, and the teachers and the board work without pay. On the contrary, it routinely faces obstacles and sanctions. The Call for Democratic Autonomy raised the demand for multiple languages, so that everyone many express themselves in their own tongue. It's been scientifically proved that languages that aren't taught can't develop further. In North Kurdistan we have Kurds, Arabs, Assyrians, Turkmens, and Armenians, and even if these groups are few, our demand is that they all be able to speak their own languages and the languages be able to develop further and be supported by the state.

What kind of connection do you have to the academies and the city council?

We work with them all. The DTK represents the whole society. We go to the meetings and work with them. One of the common projects is the construction of a language academy.

How would that work?

We would educate professional teachers, both here and in the regions. And we would research the Kurdish language at a professional level.

Which Kurdish languages are taught here now?

There are four Kurdish dialects. In North Kurdistan it's Zazaki (Dimli) and Kurmanji. When I say "Kurdish," I mean these two dialects. In South Kurdistan, Sorani and Kermanshahi are spoken. The state tries to pit Zazaki and Kurmanji speakers against each other. My friend here speaks Zazaki, while I speak Kurmanji, yet we're both in the leadership of the association.

There's no state funding, you said. How is Kurdî-Der financed?

Everything is donated. Members and sympathizers donate. They have to pay for their own transportation and food. Our teachers mostly work elsewhere-they only volunteer here. One colleague is retired and has more time.

Are the courses free?

Yes. We publish a dictionary, and selling copies brings in a little money. A participant who has no money doesn't have to pay. The voluntary subscription accounts for about 50 Turkish lira. The people come here and drink tea, and if they're doing well financially, they pay 50 lira, but that's not a precondition.

How are your offerings publicized? Word of mouth, or do you advertise?

We'd like to go door to door, but we don't have the personnel. People come of their own accord. In one class we teach twenty to thirty students, and a class lasts three months. There are three levels. After six months of study, a person can work as a teacher.

What is the gender balance in the Kurdish classes? And among the teachers?

Among the teachers it's equal. Among the classes it varies, and we don't keep statistics. Whoever shows up is accepted.

Do the participants have to be able to read and write?

That's necessary. We're talking with the city government about offering literacy classes, for example to older women, in which Kurdish will be taught too. Also people come to us from around the region who would like to learn Kurdish. A small number of Turkish doctors, teachers, and caregivers from western Turkey come here.

The Turkish state operates a Kurdish TV network. Are there also state-run Kurdish courses?

There is TRT6, but its goal isn't to develop the Kurdish language, but to allow it to rot: it broadcasts state propaganda in Kurdish, followed only by music. Sixty contemporary Kurdish concepts are forbidden to be mentioned on TRT6. Many people who were initially filled with hope about TRT6 have been disappointed, and many who worked there have left the broadcaster. The state doesn't accept the Kurdish language as an official language; it sees it as only a local dialect. During the elections, TRT6 disseminated AKP propaganda among the Kurds and oppressed the Kurdish freedom movement. This broadcaster has no guaranteed rights and can be banned by the broadcasting company RTUK at any time, because of the Kurdish language!

There's another network that partly broadcasts in Kurdish, Dünya TV, from the Gülen community. Its goal is to send Islamic propaganda into Kurdish households. If we collect ten children here to teach them Kurdish, the state prosecutor will come around in a second. But on every street corner, there's a Koran school—they're propaganda sites of the AKP and the Gülen movement. Formerly a child had to be twelve years old to attend a Koran course, but now the age of entry has been lowered to seven.

Can't Koran courses be offered in Kurdish? The imam is close to the movement, isn't he?

Maybe in the movement such considerations are discussed. A few Kurdish activists are believers, but I'm not. I don't find it good to copy the praxis of the AKP. In fact, I'm opposed to it. Religious instruction must always be conducted on a voluntary basis. To force seven-year-olds to do it—that obviously has nothing to do with free will. Moreover even for the teaching of religion, certain standards that have to be met.

How do you motivate children to speak their native tongue?

We encourage parents to speak Kurdish at home with their children. We also try to build kindergartens in which Kurdish is taught to preschoolers. That's a plan, but there are still legal difficulties. In the 1960s to the 1990s, many boarding schools were established in Kurdistan, in order to detach the children at a young age from their families and to "Turkify" them.

Are there books and movies for children and youth in Kurdish?

They exist, but unfortunately only a few. We're trying to change that. People who can read Turkish can't automatically read Kurdish—it has to be studied. So most Kurdish children read Turkish children's books. TRT6 shows no children's movies, although Roj TV does. But the Turkish state is trying to ban even these networks. Every three months we publish a journal to advance the language, which is directed at children. "Play of Fire" was the name of the first edition, named after a Kurdish game. The name didn't sound so good, so we changed it to "Children of the Sun."

What's the content of the magazine?

It contains children's fairy tales, stories of the wolf and the donkey, but also articles about Amed, short stories, children's jokes, the history of the Kurdish alphabet, and explanations of how to study it. The magazine is aimed at children as much as adults, who read from it aloud.

What associations for cultivating the language exist, and what kind of collaborative work do they do?

We work with The Movement for Kurdish Education and Language, TZP-Kurdî.[9] The Kurdish Institute has its base in this building, but it works more on linguistics and publishes books. Additionally there's also the Union of Kurdish Writers. Those are the language institutions, all work under the aegis of the TZP-Kurdî.

We'd like to know more about the tradition of dengbêj. Do you think the tales that are so transmitted should be written down?

Kurdish for along time was not a written language, it was only spoken. So the dengbêj speak-singers and fairy tale tellers are very important for us. Earlier they came to the villages and taught the children. Then the whole village would come together, sometimes for an entire night. So language and culture and life were preserved. Then the language was ruthlessly suppressed, bludgeoned. When someone from the village went to the bazaar in the city in order to sell his wares, he was fined for every Kurdish word he spoke. Because the people went on speaking Kurdish anyway, the whole day's income could go to pay for

---

9   Tevgera Ziman û Perwerdehiya Kurdî, TZP-Kurdî.

the fines. Today assimilation is more subtle, more institutional—and so Kurdish has to be taught in lessons.

Some young Kurds in the big cities hardly know any Kurdish and so doubt their Kurdish identity. What do you think about the situation in the metropolises, where the Turkish language is so massively dominant?

That's a problem. Young people's anti-Kurdish consciousness is a wildfire that poses a great danger for Kurdish culture. Dêrsim, for one, is already pretty much assimilated. The assimilation policy is knocking on the city walls of Amed. In the 1990s, during the war, four thousand villages were evacuated, so people here have awareness of being Kurdish because of that. But yes, the language is losing meaning, as ever more Turkish is spoken. So Kurdish simply must be taught in classes. Language is more than a means of communication—it is also formative of identity.

Are there other language associations, for example Armenian, and if so, do you have an exchange with them?

There are no other language associations, and we can't teach other languages. But we're trying to support the cultures of the other minorities and so to preserve cultural diversity. In Amed, for example, churches are being restored. In the DTK the other minorities are represented, and recently they took part in a Kurdistan conference here. Yes, the state's assimilation policy applies to all minorities, not just the Kurds. Thirty years go a Christian or an Armenian could not adhere to their identity. Whether we like it or not, the struggle of the PKK has changed that. Now minorities can stand up for themselves. That's an achievement of the resistance.

Glossary

Academy: In Democratic Confederalism, academies are the center of the independent education movement. They hold discussion forums for the people in city neighborhoods, and they offer up to three month long seminars for movement activists. In North Kurdistan now there are thirteen academies with various foci, for example, general political academies, women's academies, and academies for religion and culture.

Abdullah Öcalan: Born in 1948, Öcalan (often called Apo) is the founder and former head of the Kurdistan Workers Party, PKK. Since 1999 he has been in solitary confinement at the prison island Imrali. In the summer of 2009 he issued a "Road Map" for the democratization of Turkey and for the peaceful and political solution of the Kurdish question. The essential ideas and impetus for the Democratic Confederalism came from him.

AKP: The Justice and Development Party (Adalet ve Kalkınma Partisi) was founded in 2001 by Recep Tayyip Erdoğan. Islamic conservative in nature, it has ruled Turkey since 2002 with an absolute majority. It tries to convey an impression of being a reform policy and of wishing for a "democratic opening," but during its tenure it has brought many state institutions, including the military and justice, under its control and has built up the strength of the police by means of the 1995 Anti-Terror Law. Ideologically and personally, the AKP is tied closely to he Islamic nationalist, neoliberal-oriented Fetullah Gülen movement.

BDP: The Peace and Democracy Party (Barış ve Demokrasi Partisi) is leftist and pro-Kurdish. It was founded in 2008 shortly before the banning of the similarly pro-Kurdish Party for Democratic Society (DTP). In the parliamentary elections of June 2001 the BDP joined with other parties to form the electoral coalition Labor, Democracy, and Freedom Bloc (Emek, Demokrasi ve Özgürlük Bloku) and supported independent candidates, among others from the Turkish left. At the time thirty-six delegates were elected to the Turkish parliament. At this writing (July 2012), six of the delegates are in prison.

Committees: Within the DTK and in the councils, the committees handle the various work areas. They are, among others, committees on economics, women, ecology, religion, law, education, youth, and the Kurdish language.

Councils: The construction of grassroots-organized, self-managing communes is the focus of the reorganized Kurdish movement. For the past few years in all regions of the Kurdish areas city, neighborhood, street, and village councils have been founded. Since July 2011, with the program of Democratic Autonomy, the organization of councils has been strengthened. The councils organize individuals as well as representatives from popular movements, parties and civil society organizations. In these councils individuals and members of civil society organizations, associations, or institutions make up sixty percent and elected mandate holders forty percent of the delegates. There's a forty percent gender quota. The various work areas are organized in committees.

Democratic Autonomy: Democratic Autonomy, announced by the DTK on July 14, 2011, is as a step toward the democratization of all Turkey. In distinction to a state-centered concept of autonomy, which would advance communal powers, democratic participation, and self-determination from the top down, Democratic Autonomy rests on the self-organization of the people outside the state and its institutions.

Democratic Confederalism: The Democratic Confederalism social model is based on the communal self-organization of civil society. Since 2005 it has been the paradigm of the Kurdish movement. Impetus for this new orientation came from the defense writings of Abdullah Öcalan. Democratic Confederalism advocates the construction of a base-democratic council system according to the principles of gender freedom and ecology in all areas of society. In a pyramid-formed organizational model, the actual power to make decisions rests with the grassroots—that is, in the village, neighborhood, and city councils, whose delegates have a one-year term. Democratic Confederalism aims at pressing the state to make deep-seated democratic reforms and sees itself as an antistatist basis for the free cohabitation of peoples of the Middle East.

DÖKH: The Democratic Free Women's Movement (Demokratik Özgür Kadın Hareketi) was founded in 2003 by hundreds of female Kurdish activists. It brings together women from different social, cultural, and political areas, and it aims to serve as an umbrella organization to struggle against sexism, racism, nationalism, militarism, environmental destruction, and economic exploitation.

DTK: The Democratic Society Congress (Demokratik Toplum Kongresi) was founded in 2005 in Amed as a confederation of civil society organizations, political parties, and individual members of diverse ethnic, political, and religious groups. On July 14, 2011, DTK assembly of more than eight hundred participants called for Democratic Autonomy as a step toward democratization of all of Turkey. Since its founding, the DTK has been subject to vehement repression by the Turkish state.

DTP: The Democratic Society Party (Demokratik Toplum Partisi) was a leftist pro-Kurdish party that was banned in 2009. At the communal elections in March 2009, ninety-nine mayors were DTP, about double what had been before. The successor party is the Party for Peace and Democracy, the BDP.

Fetulllah Gülen movement: The imam Fetullah Gülen was born in 1941 and he now lives in the United States. His movement is the most influential Islamic tendency in Turkey. It is nationalist and neoliberal oriented. Part of the Gülen movement is a worldwide network of education institutions, media, and economic enterprises. Gülen's followers have honeycombed police and justice and are considered responsible for the recent mass arrests of Kurdish oppositionists, government-critical journalists, and high military figures. Gülen calls for the military annihilation of the Kurdish freedom movement and wants the Sunni Kurds to assimilate and to reconcile with the Turkish state, according to the Ottoman model, in the name of Islam.

KCK: The Union of Kurdistan Communities (Koma Civakên Kurdistanê) is a grassroots political umbrella organization that advocates the implementation of Democratic Confederalism.

PKK: the Workers Party of Kurdistan (Partiya Karkerên Kurdistan) was founded in 1978, and Abdullah Öcalan was elected head. The PKK's goal was the construction of an independent, unified, socialist Kurdistan. It was a Marxist-Leninist party. In 1984 it declared armed struggle. In 2002 the PKK dissolved itself and was re-founded anew in the framework of a new paradigm: Democratic Confederalism, the construction of a democratic, ecological, and gender-liberated society, in Kurdistan within the KCK system. The PKK is listed as a terrorist organization by the European Union, NATO, and the United States.

Made in the USA
Charleston, SC
30 December 2013